Evvie's Compositions

by Evelyn Rea Fredericks
with Karol Ann Krakauer
Fort Collins, Colorado
2023

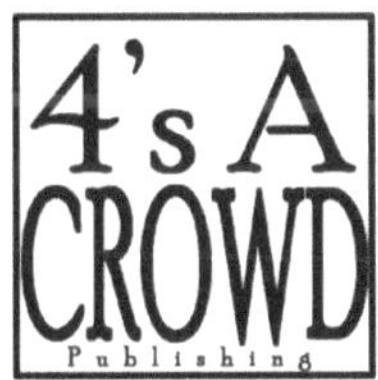

TABLE OF CONTENTS

Think Of Me

E. Fredericks

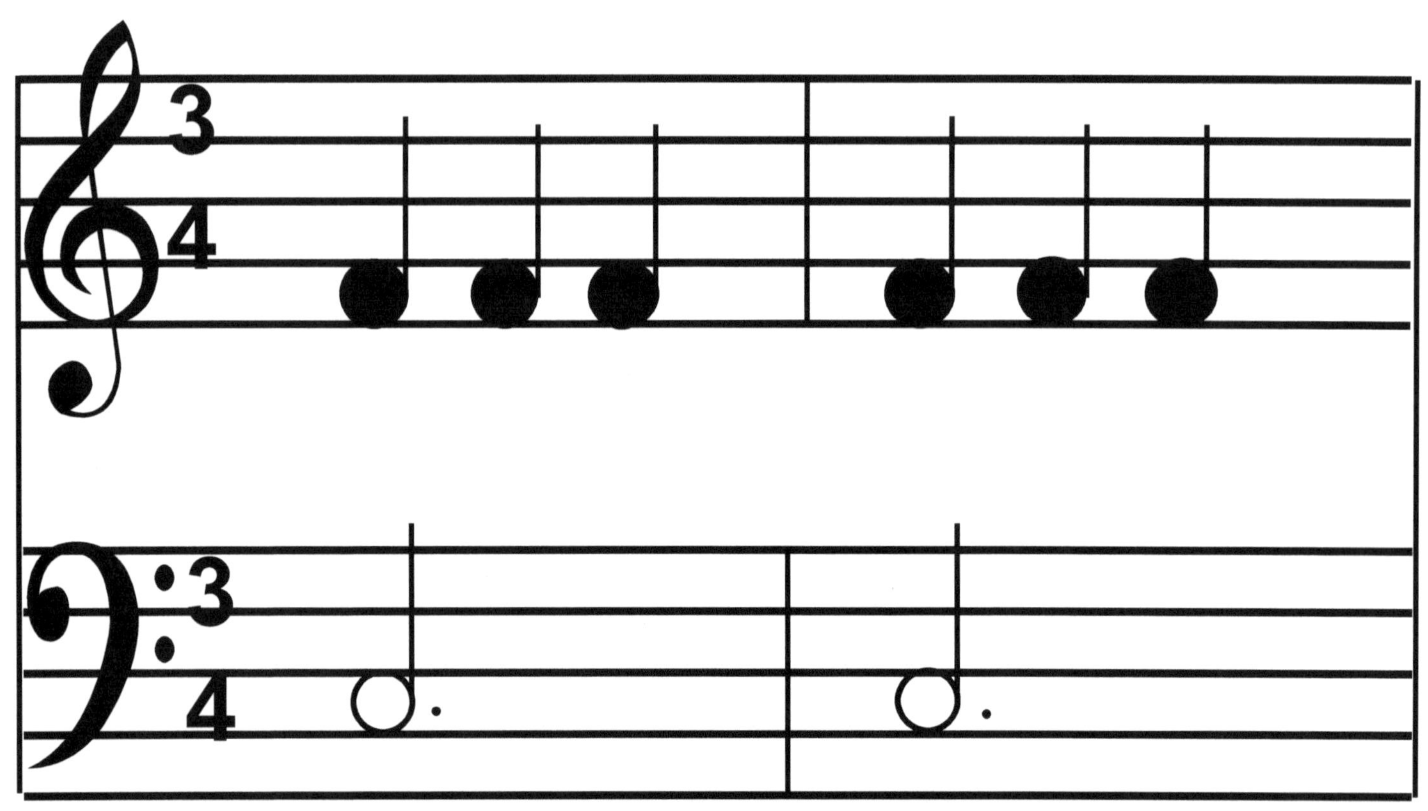

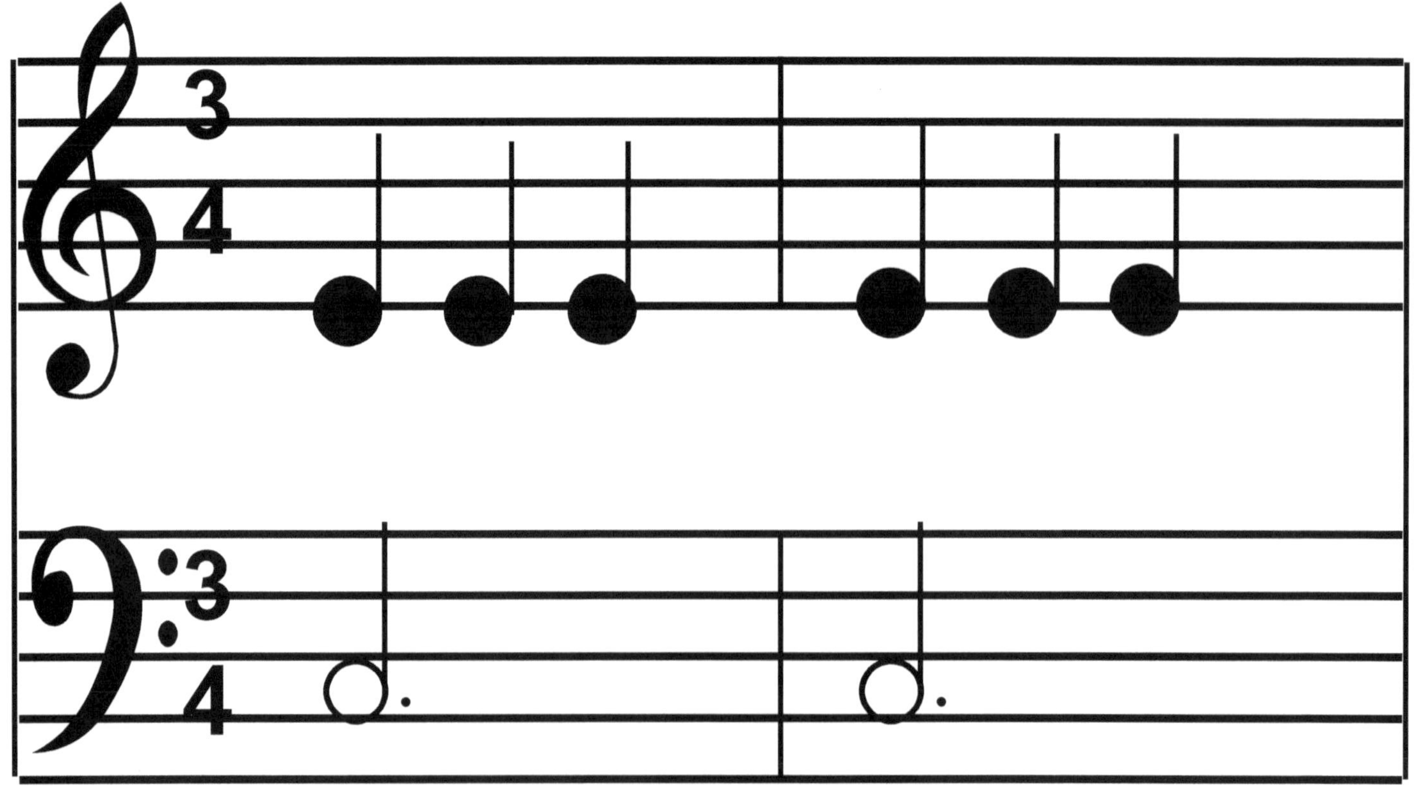

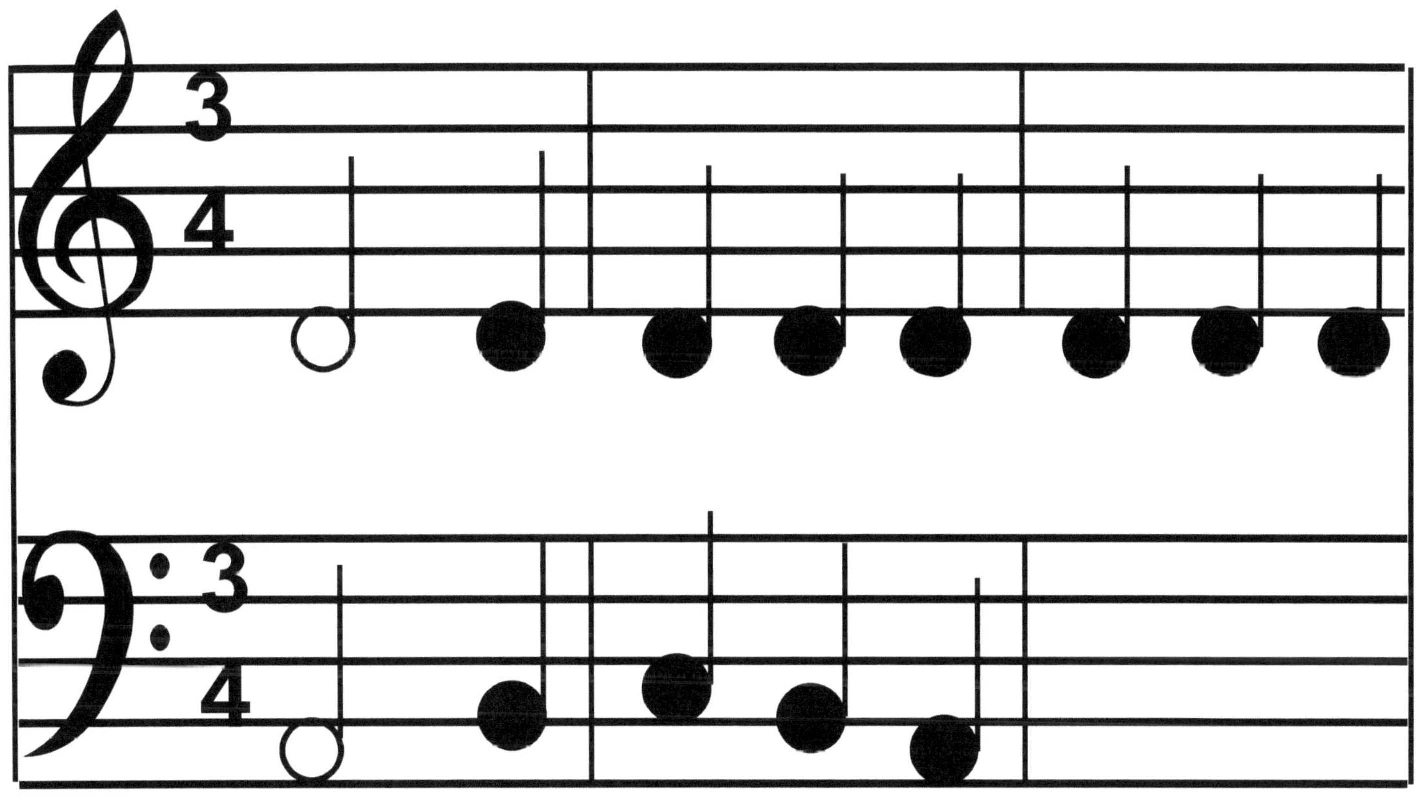

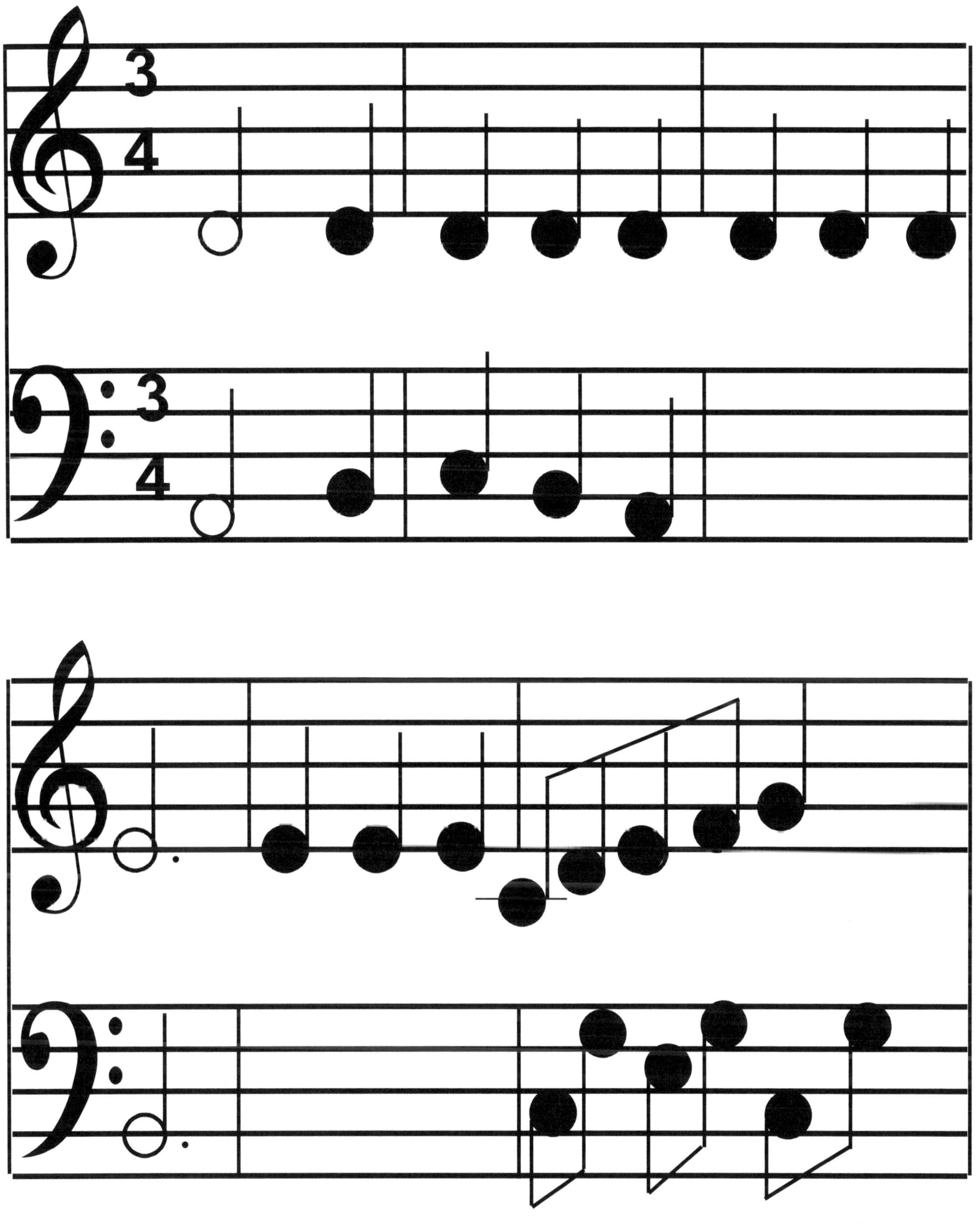

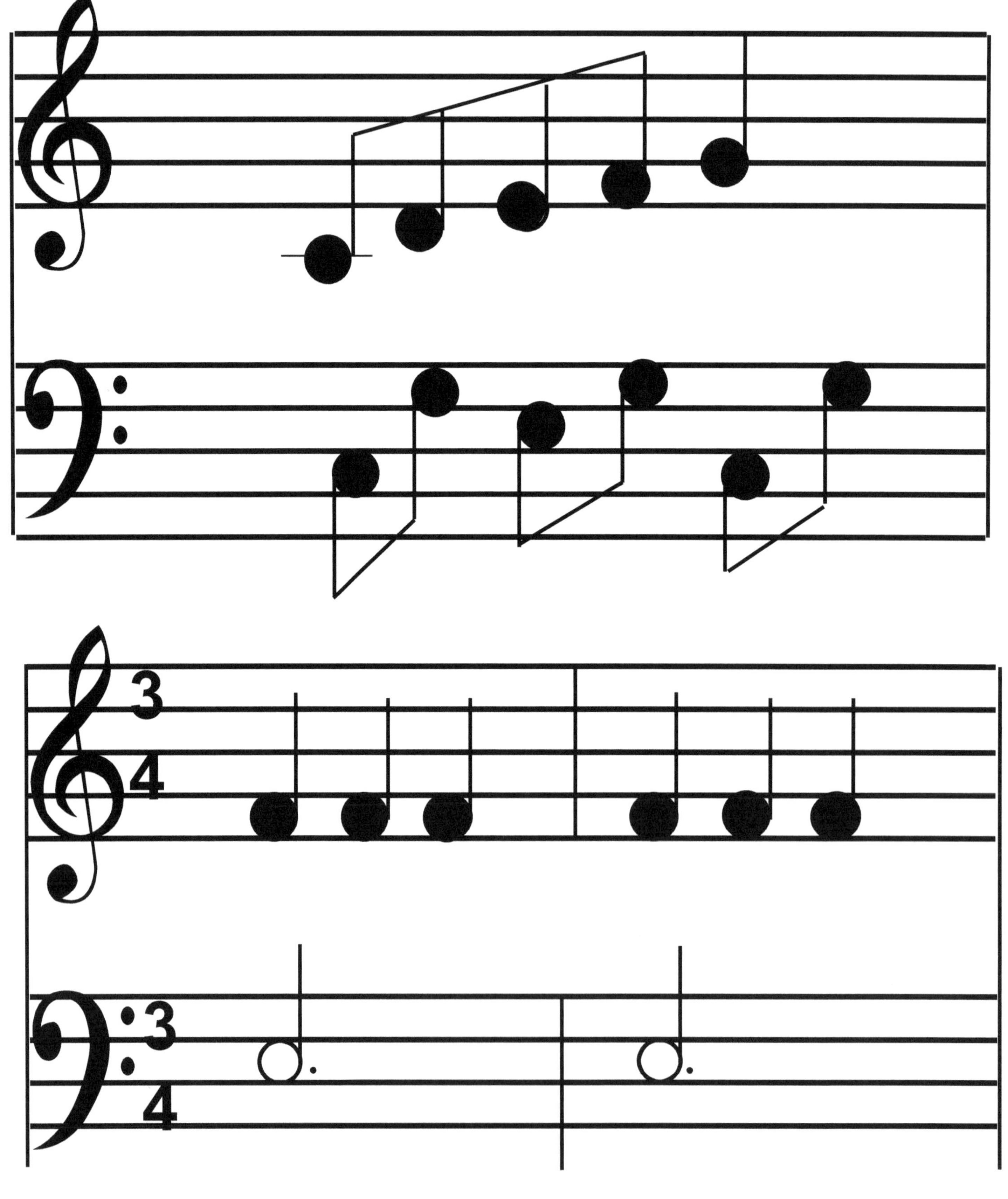

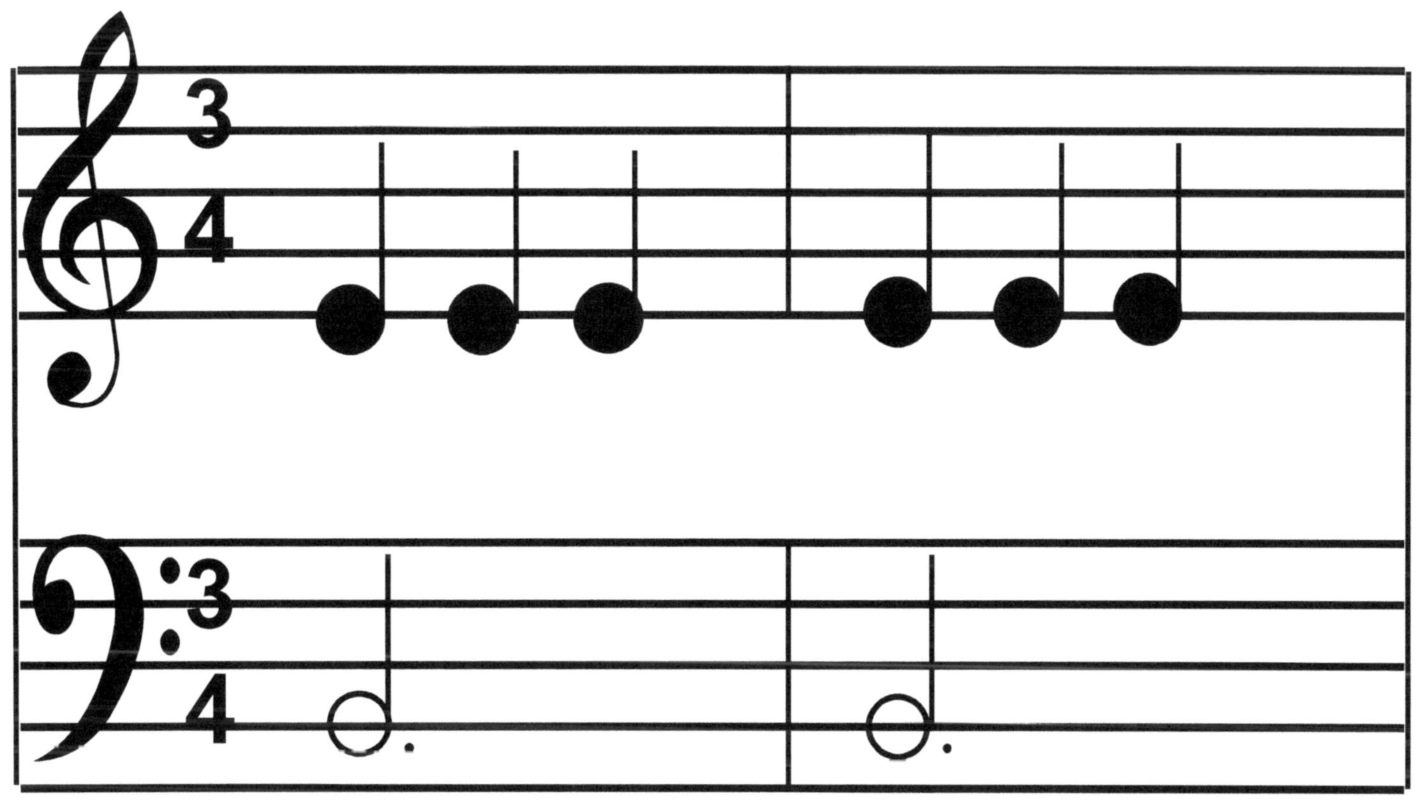

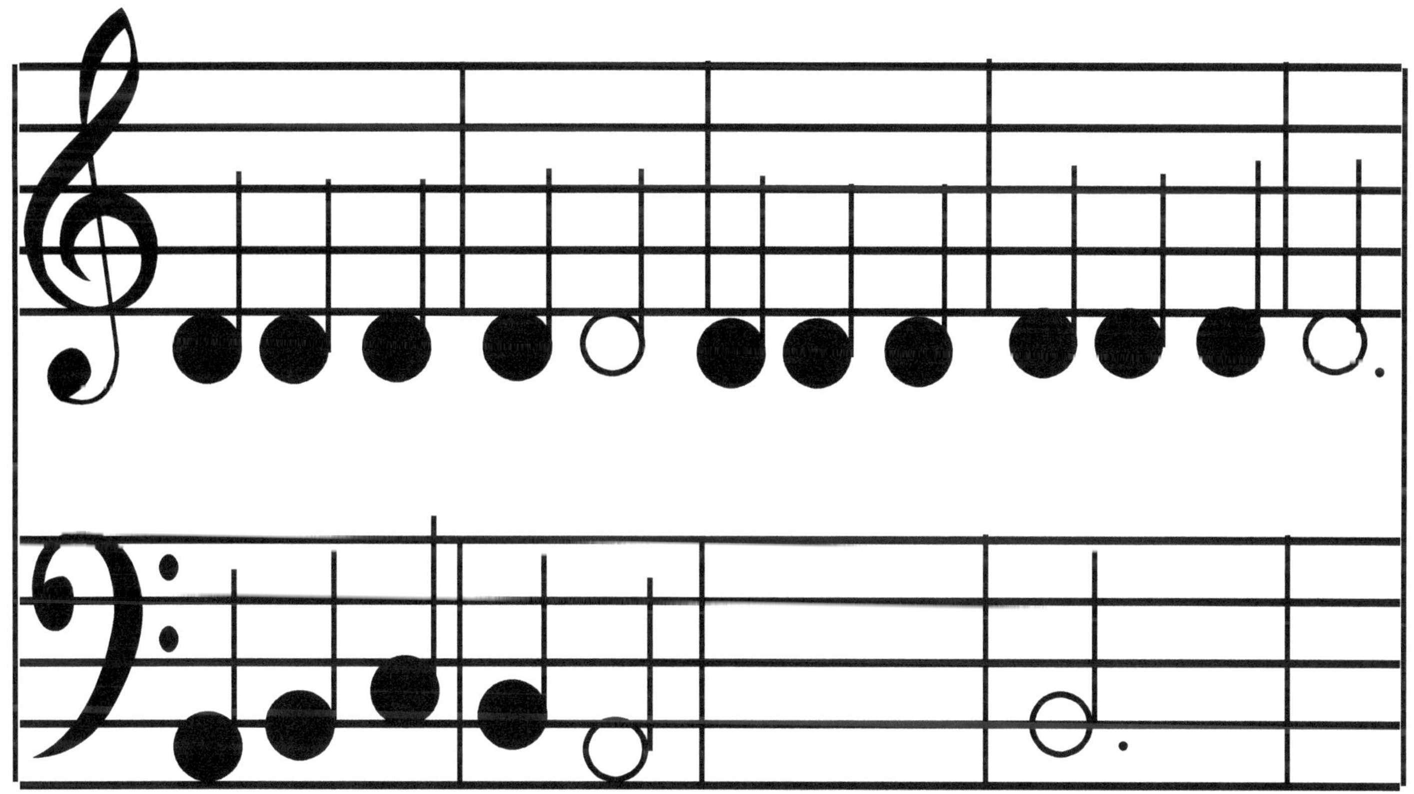

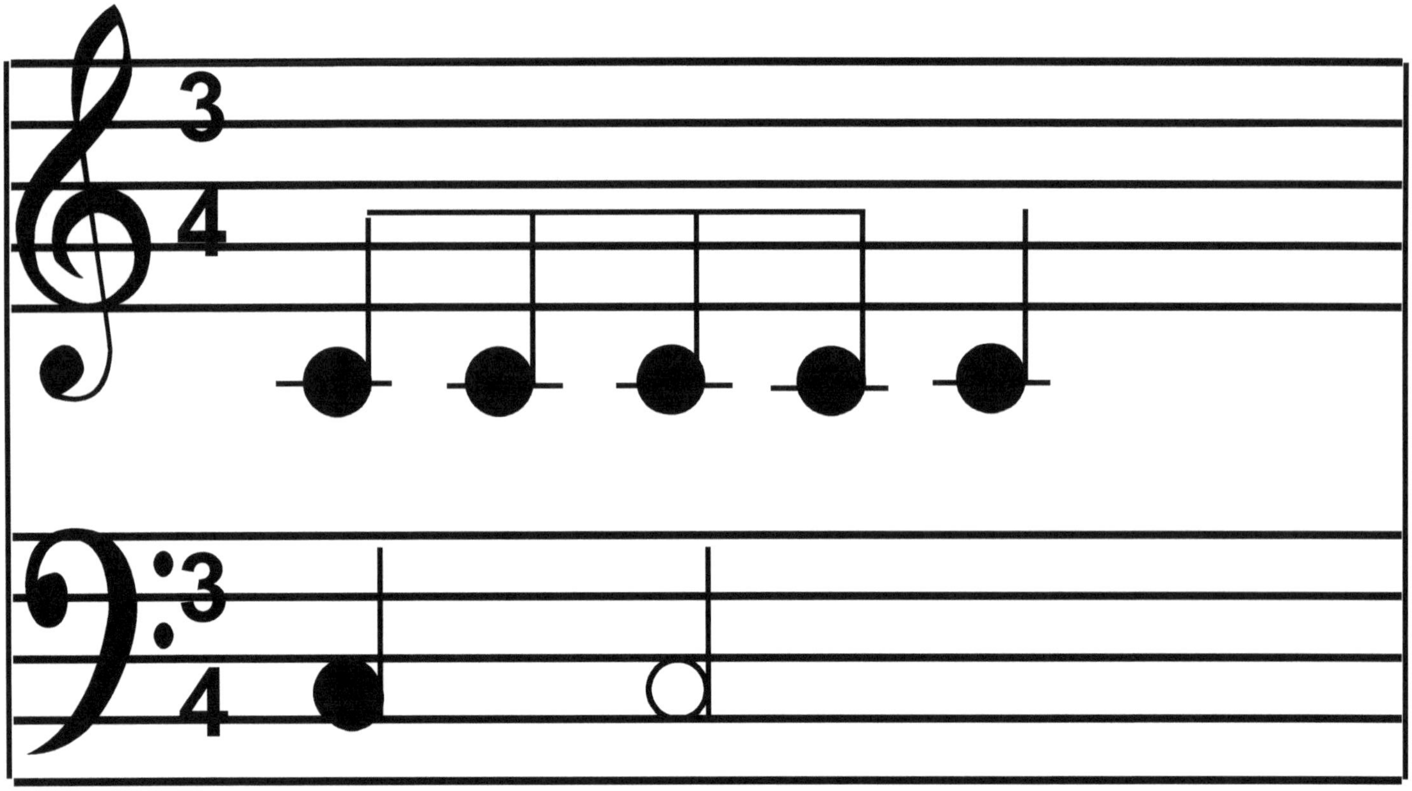

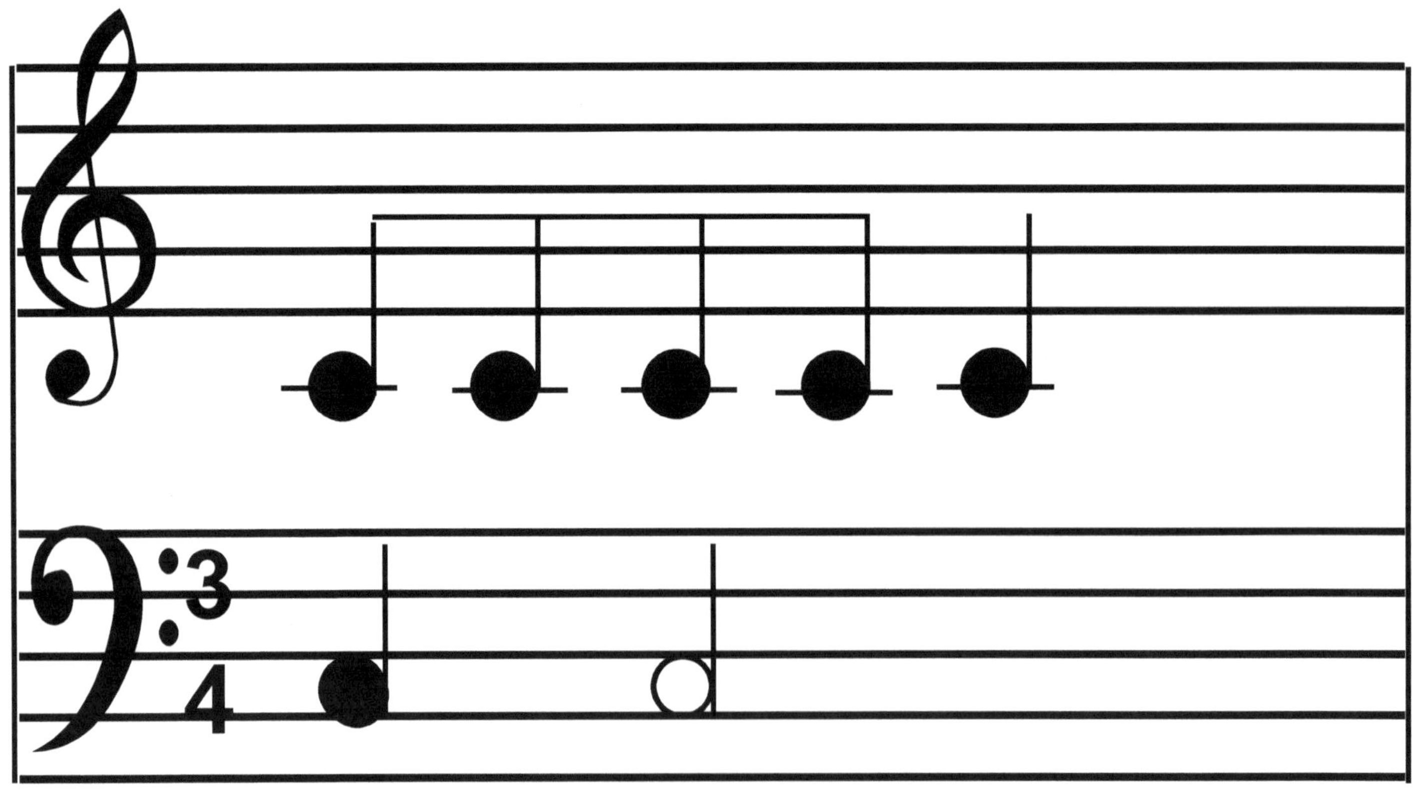

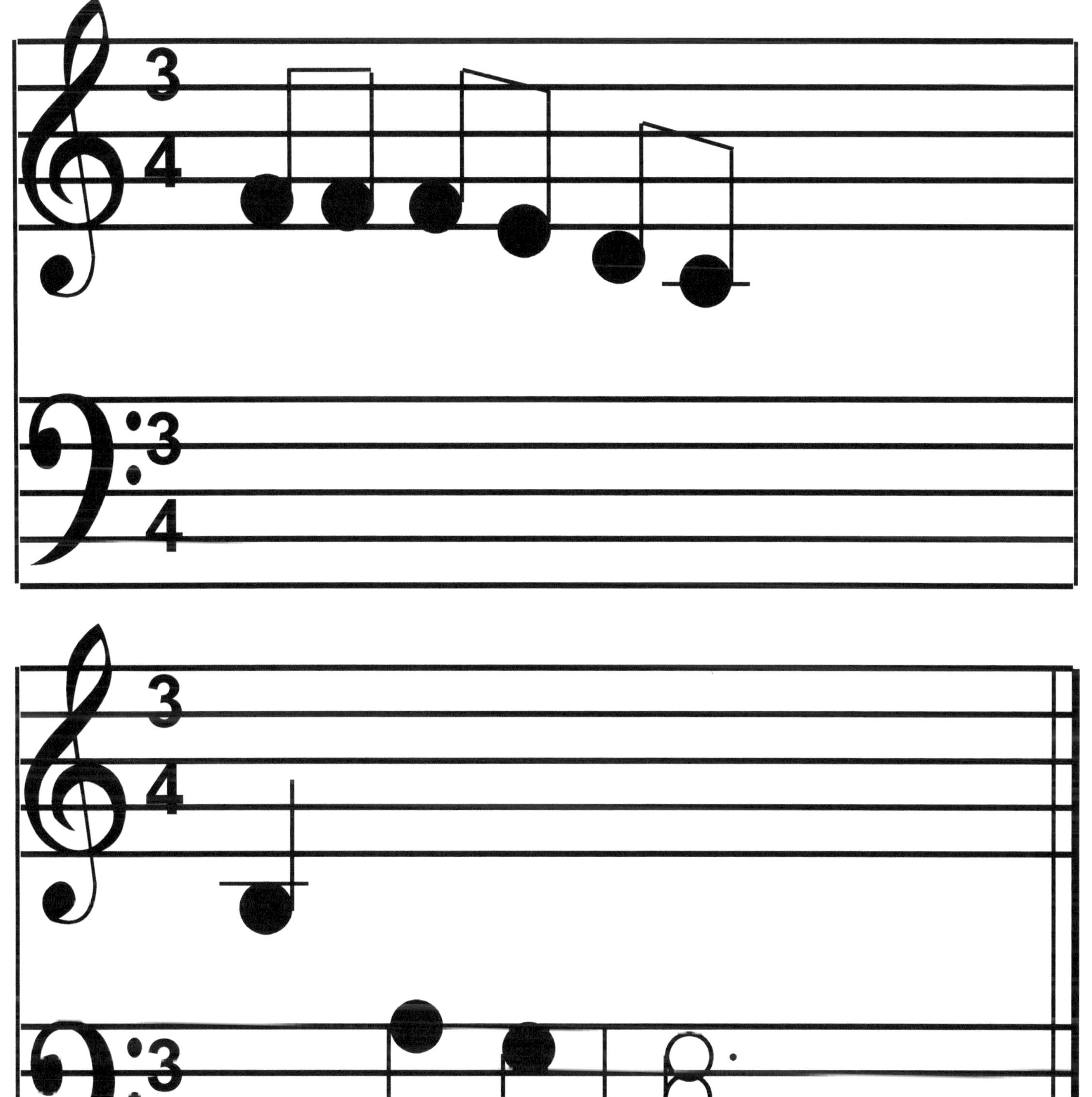

Surprise

E. Fredericks
2023

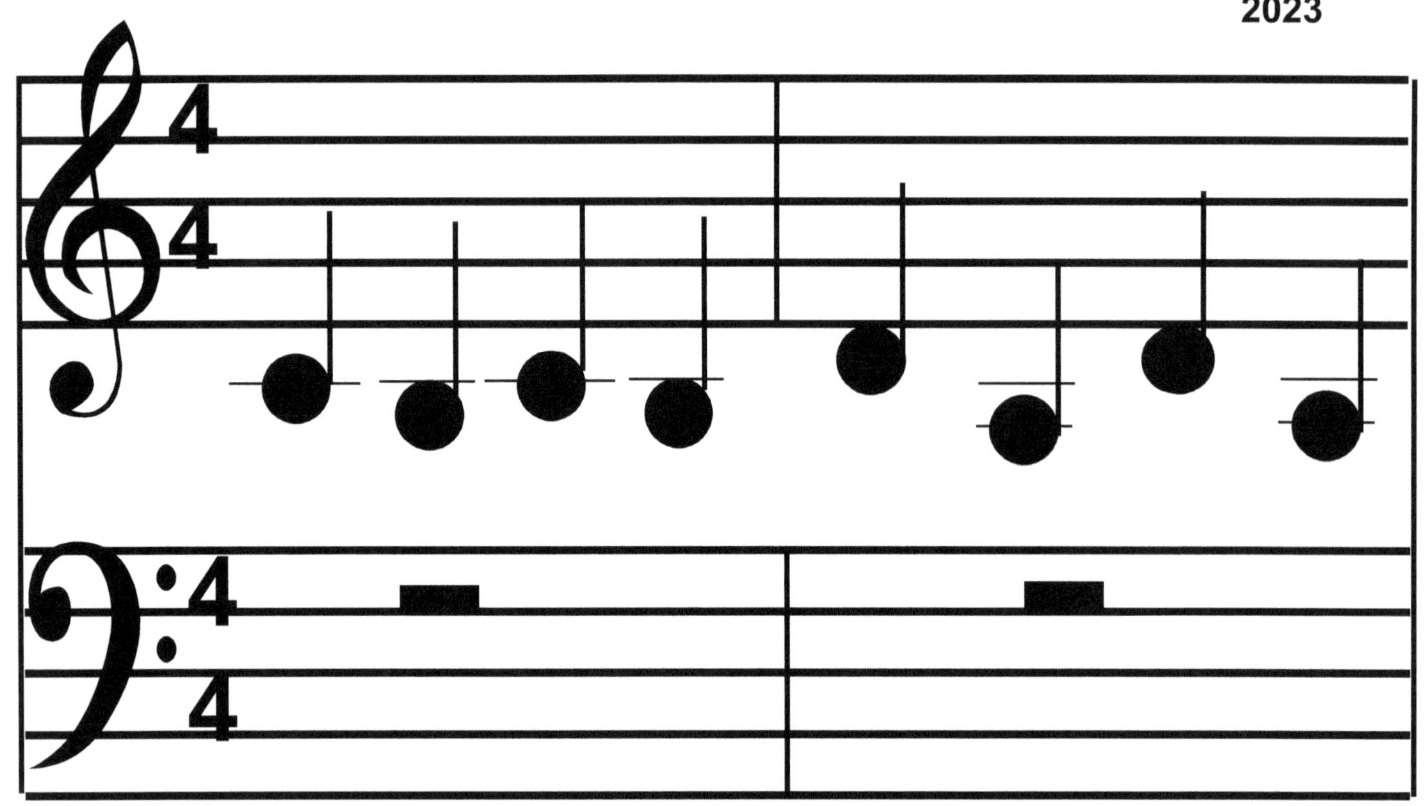

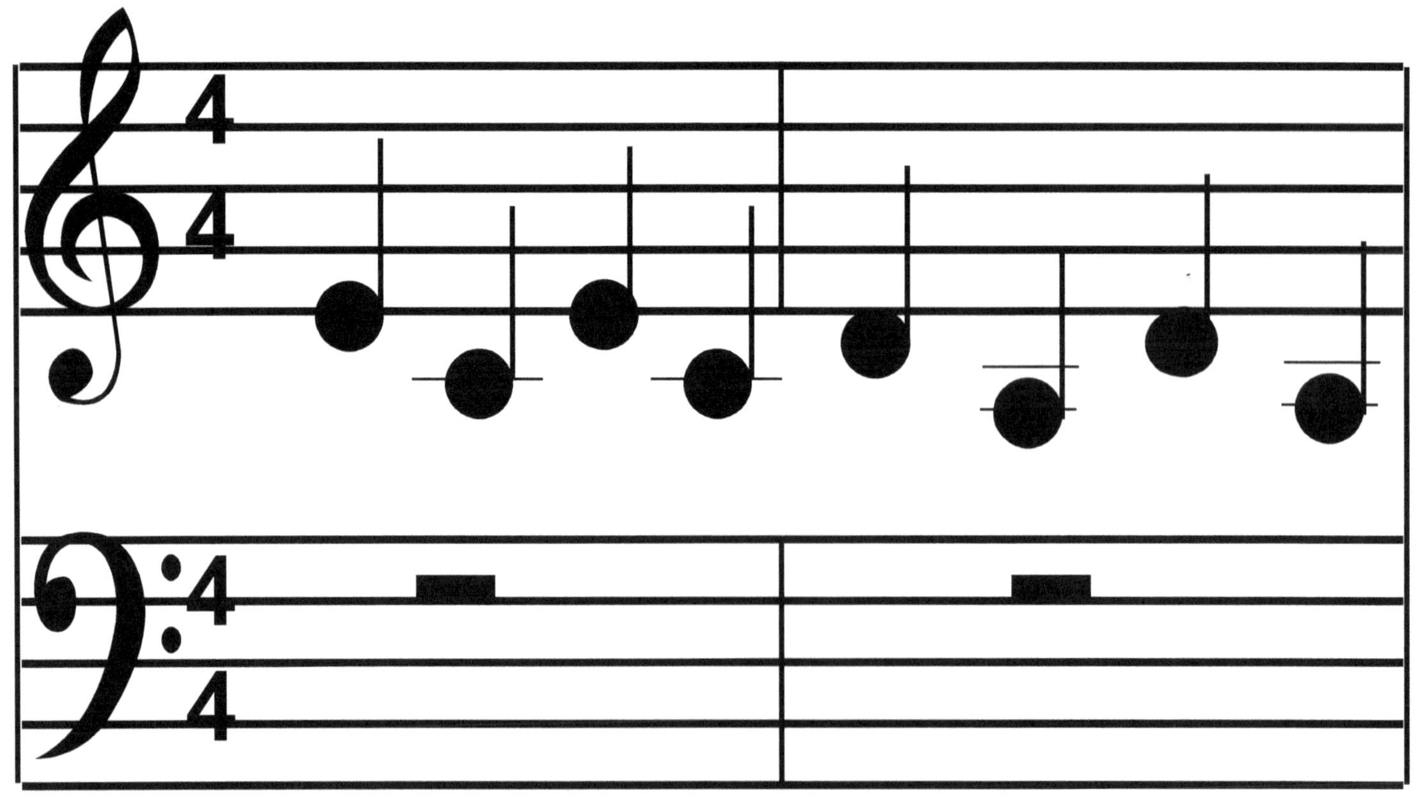

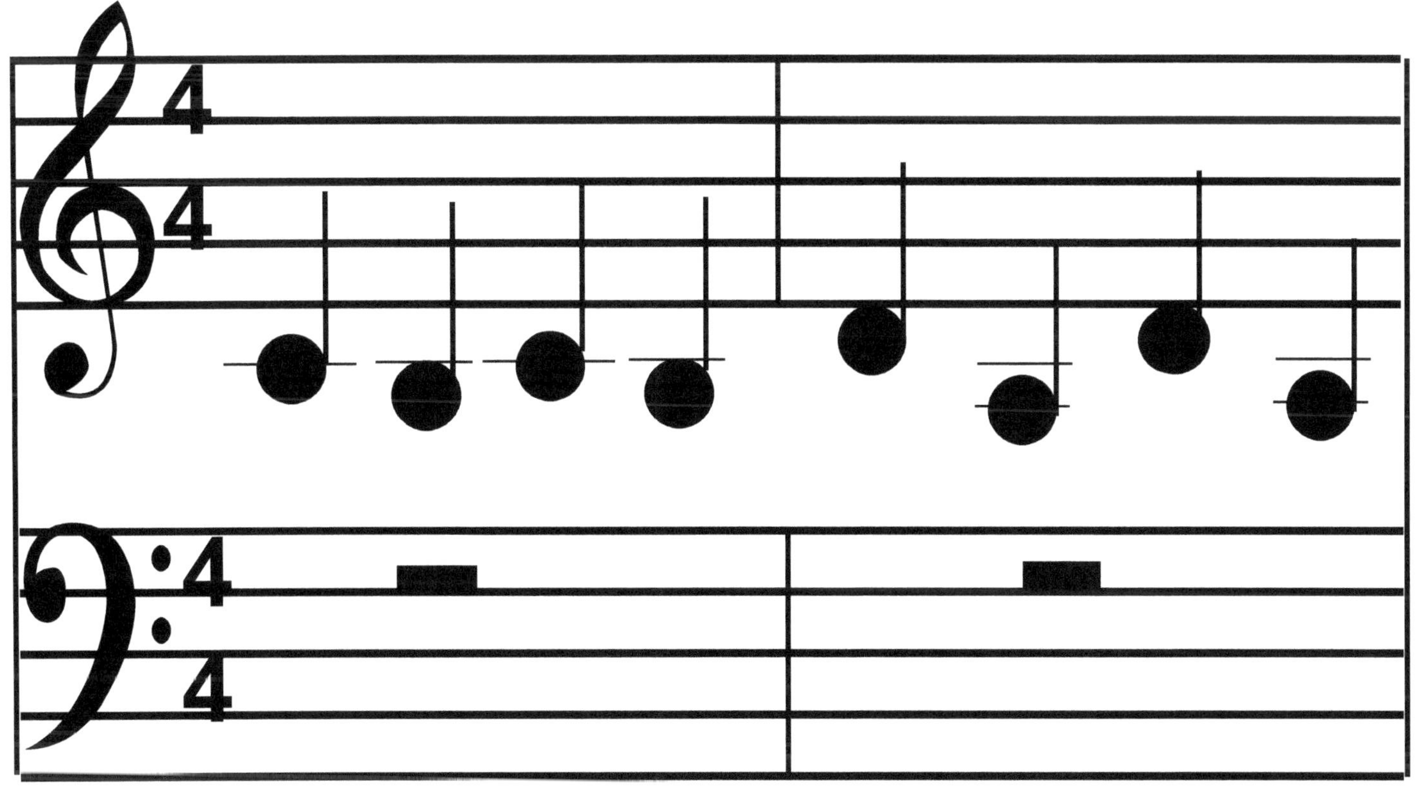

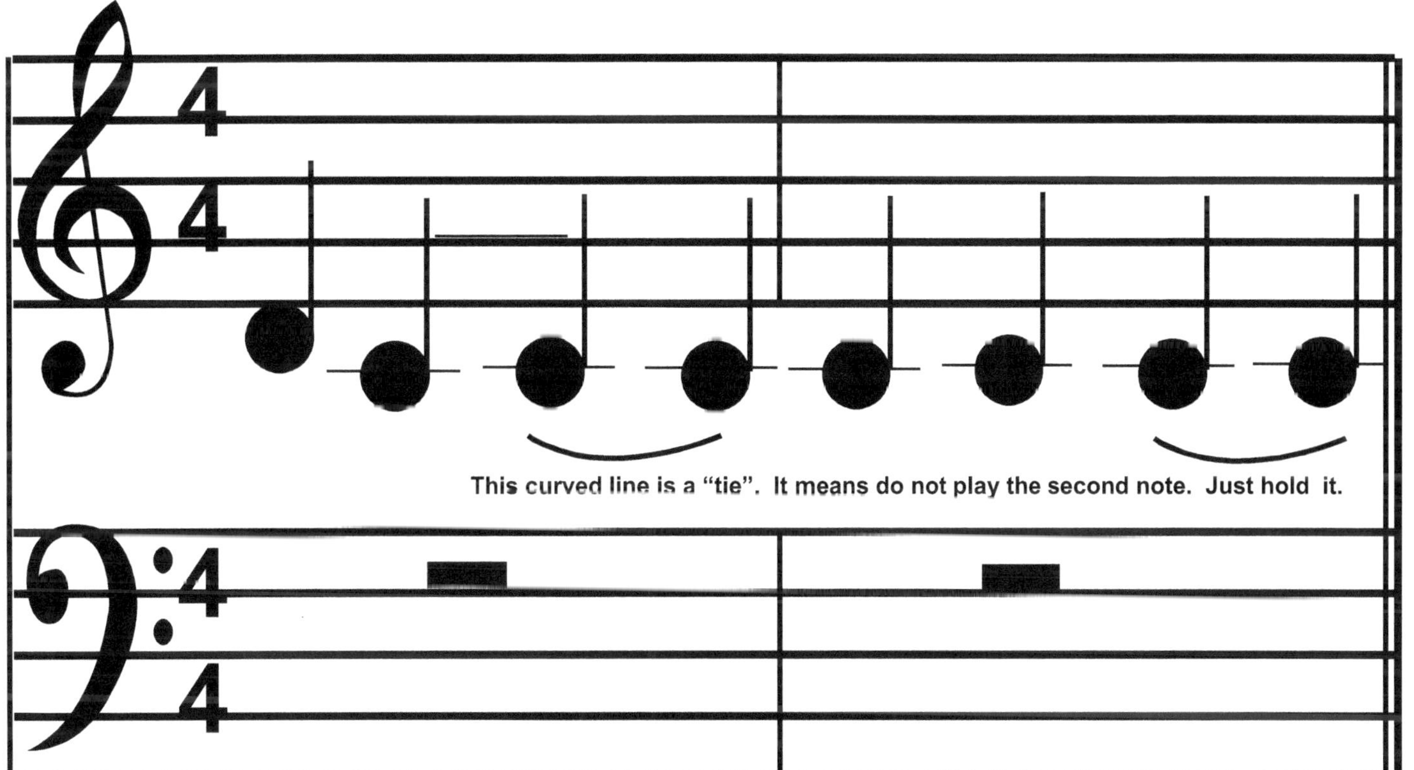
This curved line is a "tie". It means do not play the second note. Just hold it.

Counting Review

(Reprinted from Picture Songs Book 2, Scales, Chords, Fingering, Timing and Other Music Theory)

Counting is very important when you play piano.

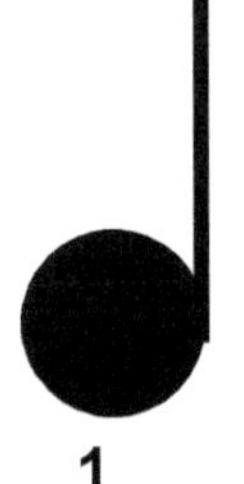

Quarter notes get 1 count.

Or 1 piece of pizza when you cut the pizza into 4 slices.

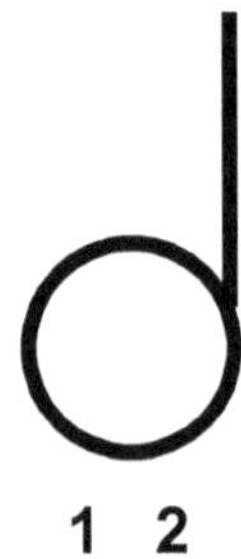

Half notes get 2 counts.

Or 2 pieces of pizza.

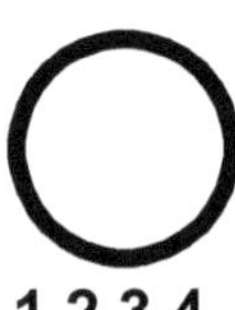

Whole notes get 4 counts.

Or all 4 pieces of pizza. Notice that whole notes have no stems.

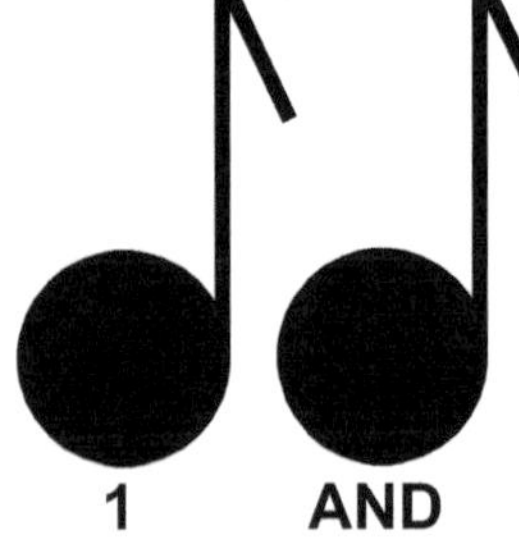

Eighth notes get 1/2 count.

You have to say "**1 AND**" when you count.

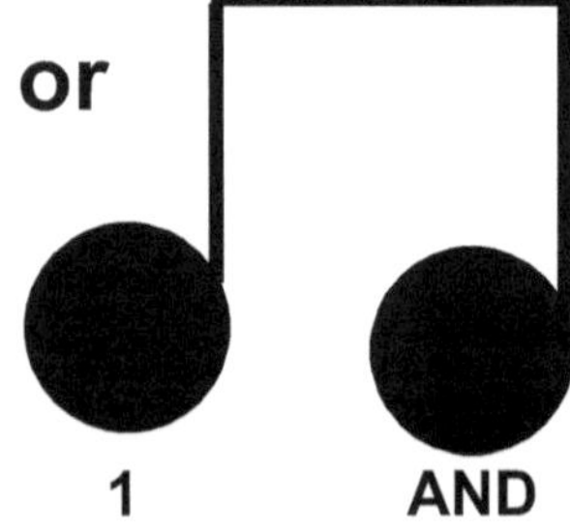

If several eighth notes are next to each other they are hooked together with a bridge.

Dots

Or chocolate drops.   Take extra time
to enjoy them.

When a "Dot" (or drop of chocolate as I call it) is placed after a note, give it extra time. (Savor the chocolate for a bit of time.) Give it its count and another half of its count also.

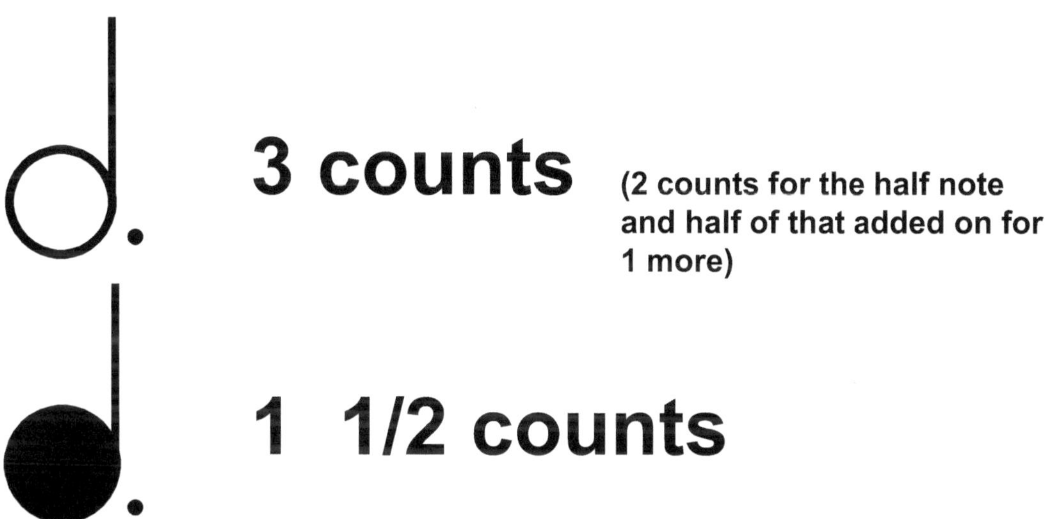

Triplets

A triplet is a group of 3 notes which have to be fit into 1 count. You say "1 trip - let" when you are counting. Be sure to give each count the same amount of time so that your rhythm is even. That may require you to count say triplet with each count so that everything matches. See the counting on the next page.

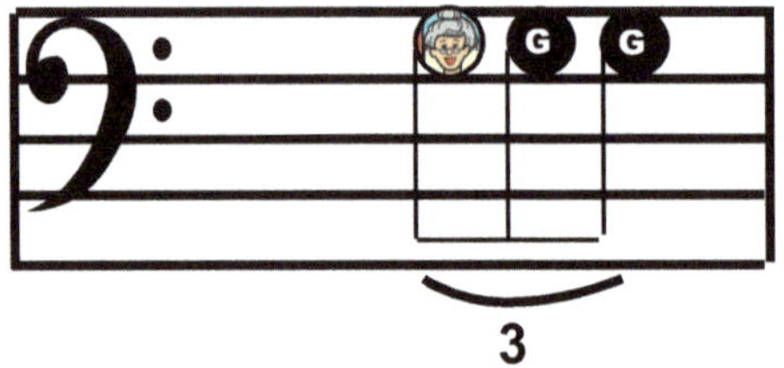

Count: 1 trip - let

Happy Times

E. Fredericks

2023

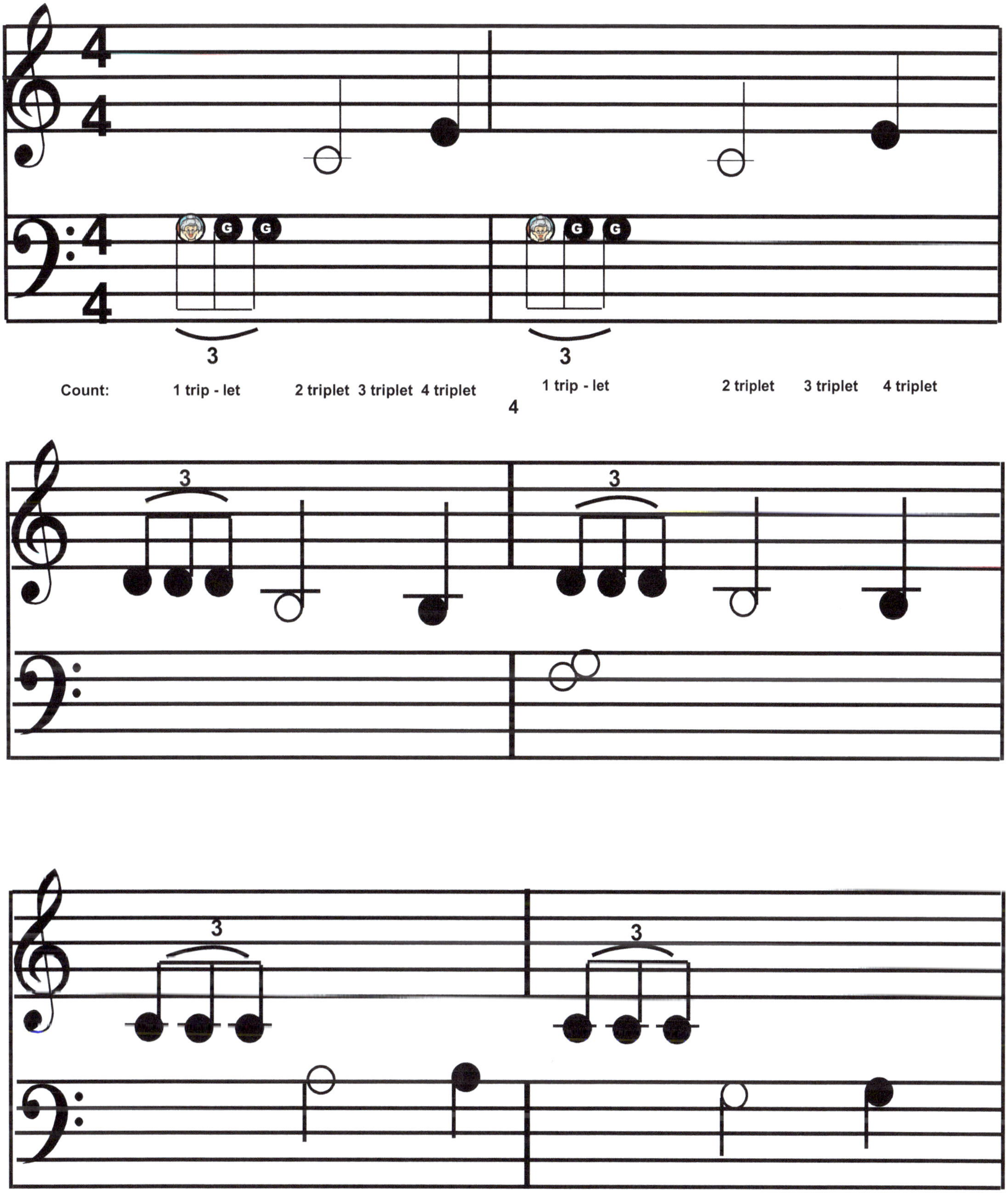

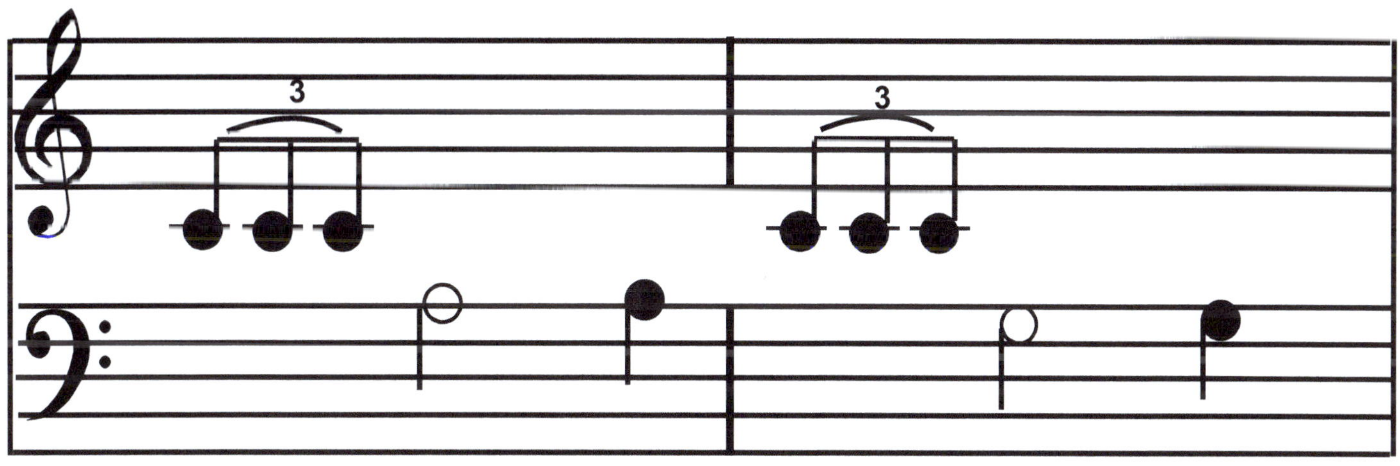

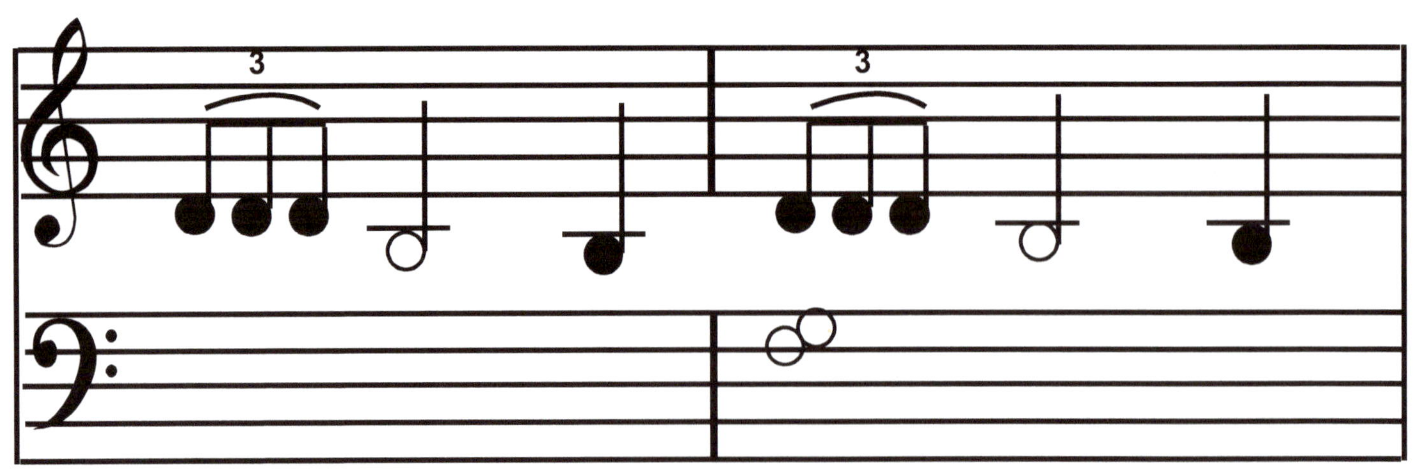

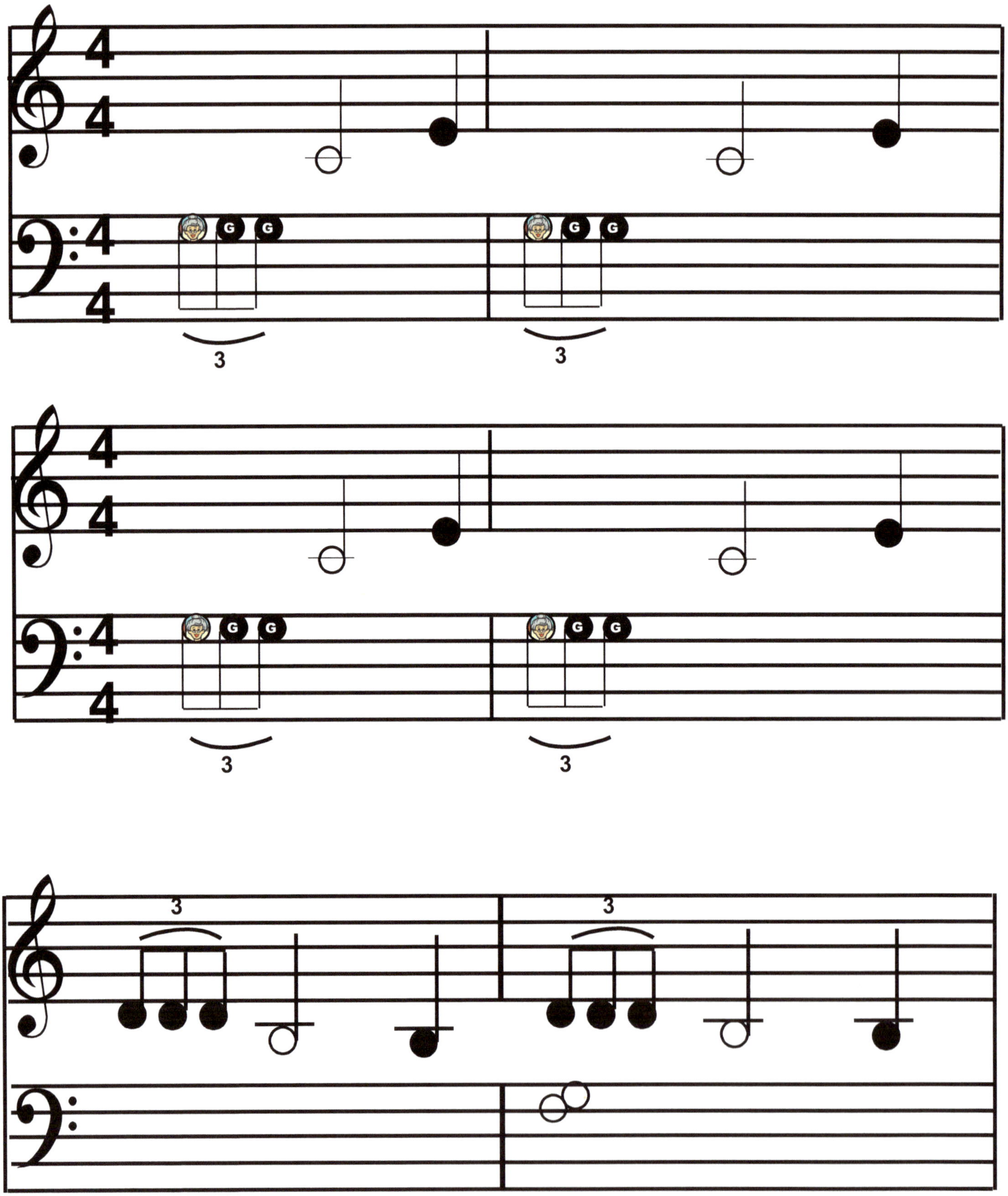

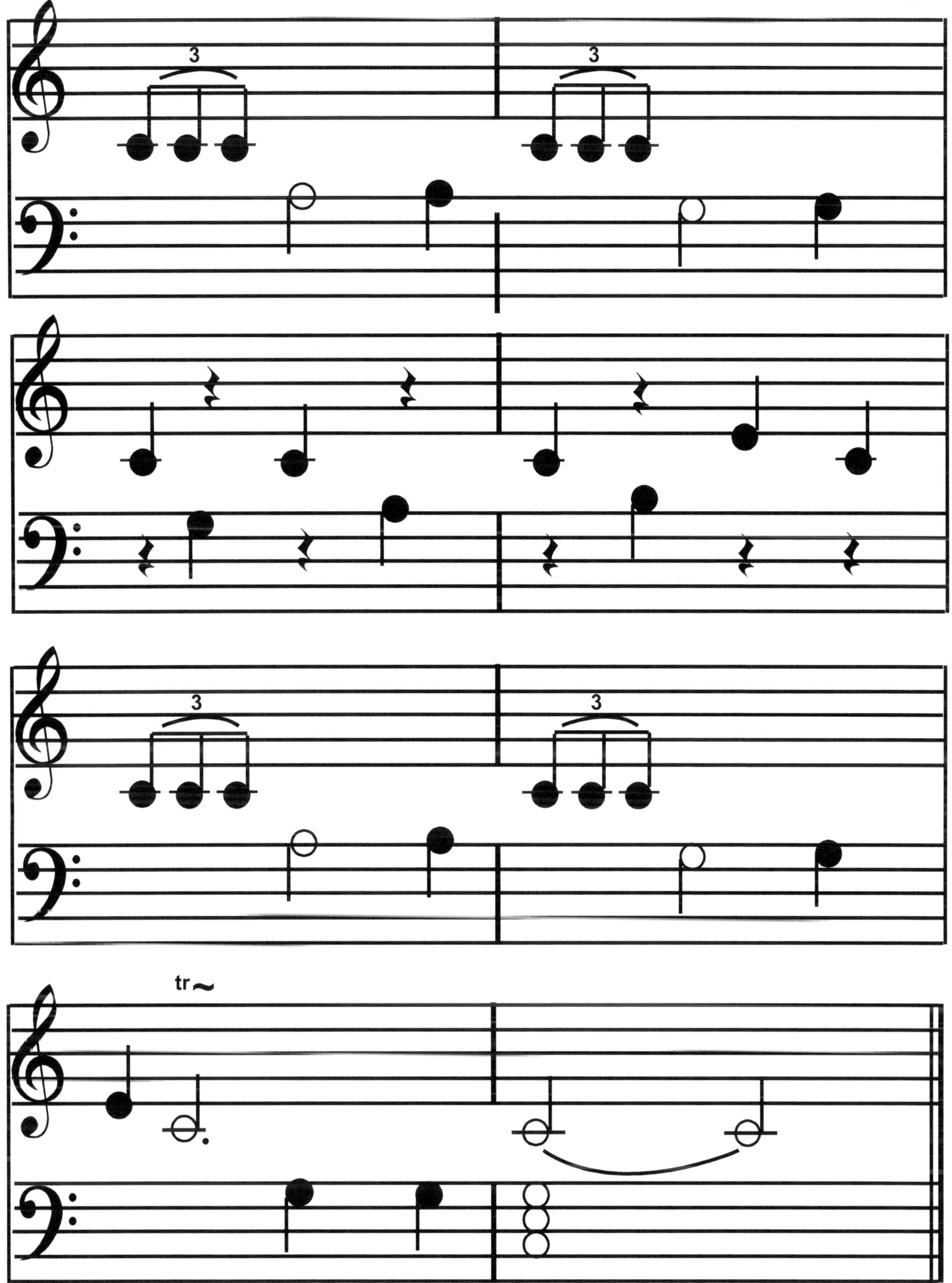
3
3
3
3
tr~

Trills and Grace Notes

In the last line of Happy Times, which you just played, you will see a trill symbol above the C in the last line. You play the note and the note above that (in the scale) back and forth as fast as you can several times. Start and end on the main note which is C here.

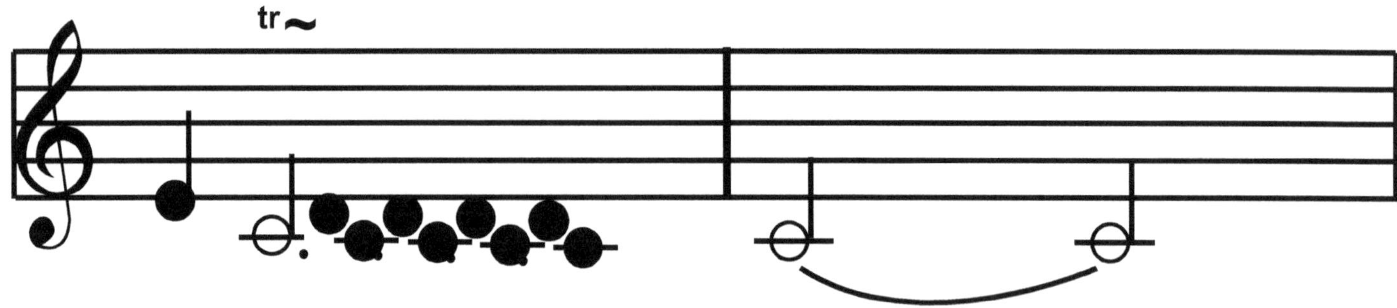

A grace note is a tiny note placed just before a main note. You play it almost at the same time as the main note but just a tiny bit before it. It is softer than the main note.

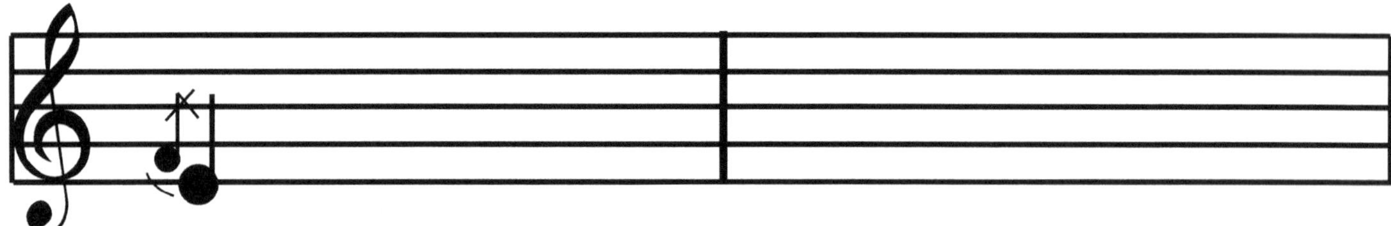

Thinking

E. Fredericks

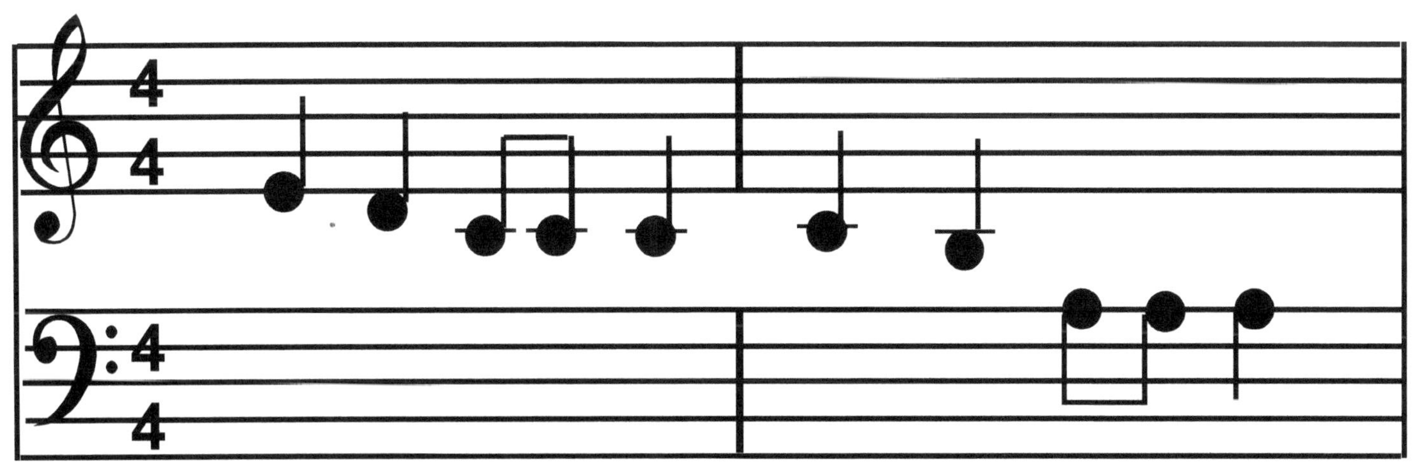

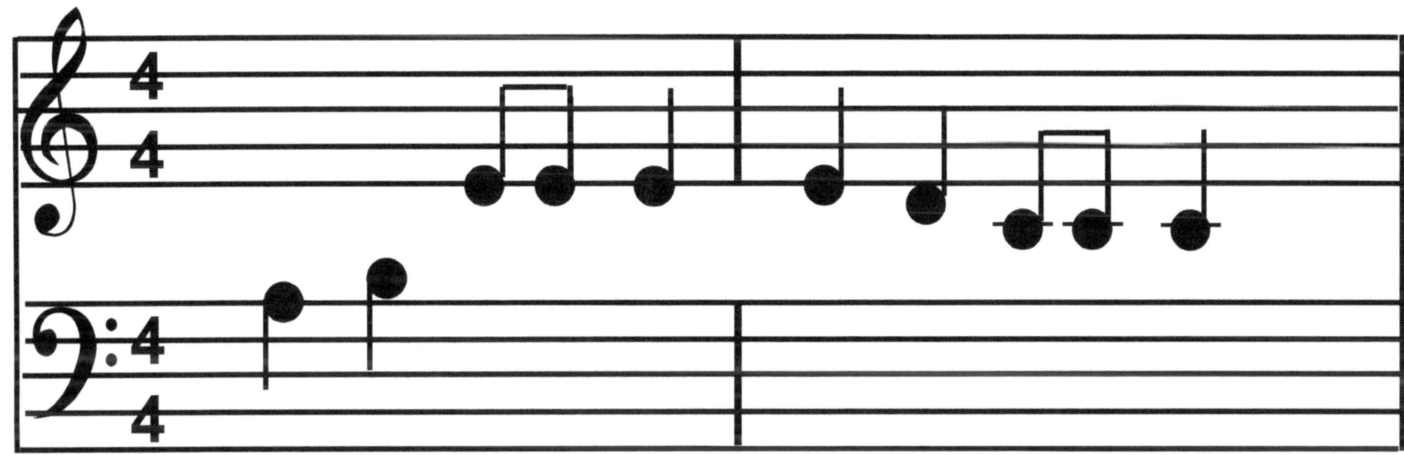

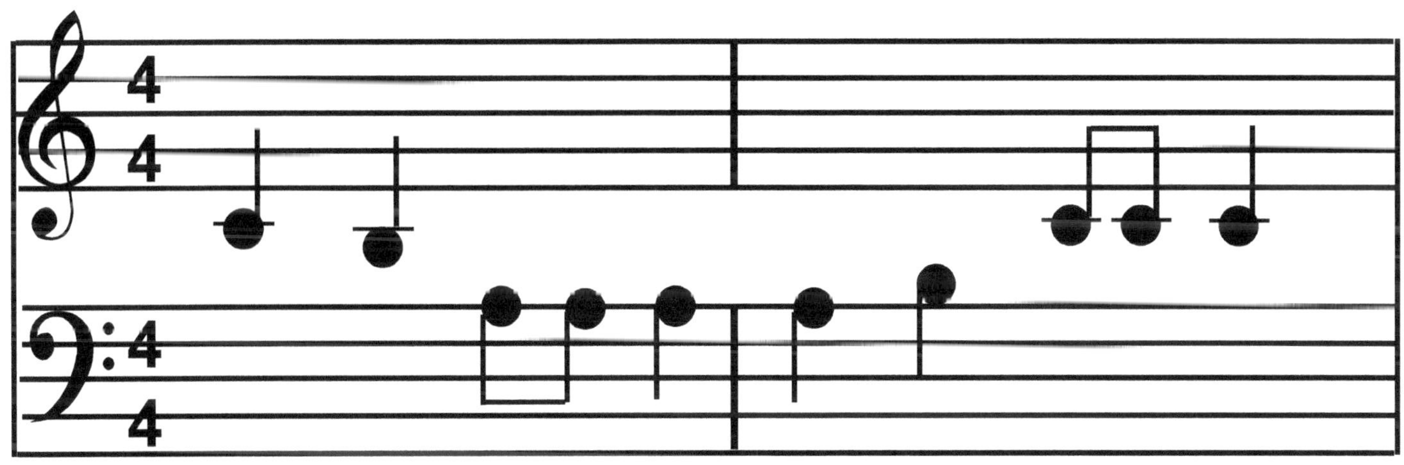

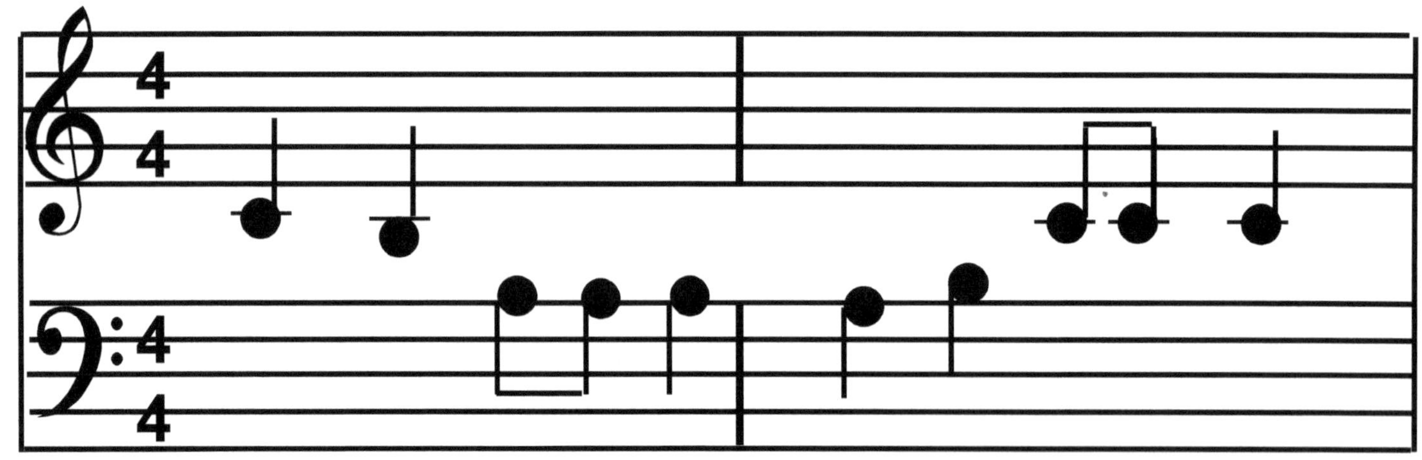

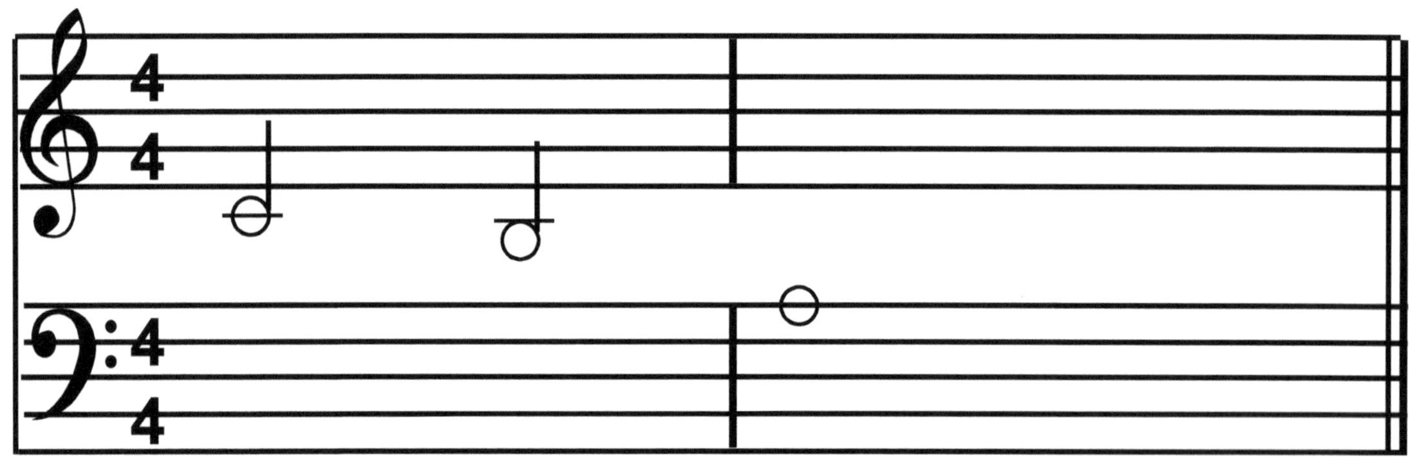

Eagles

E. Fredericks
2023

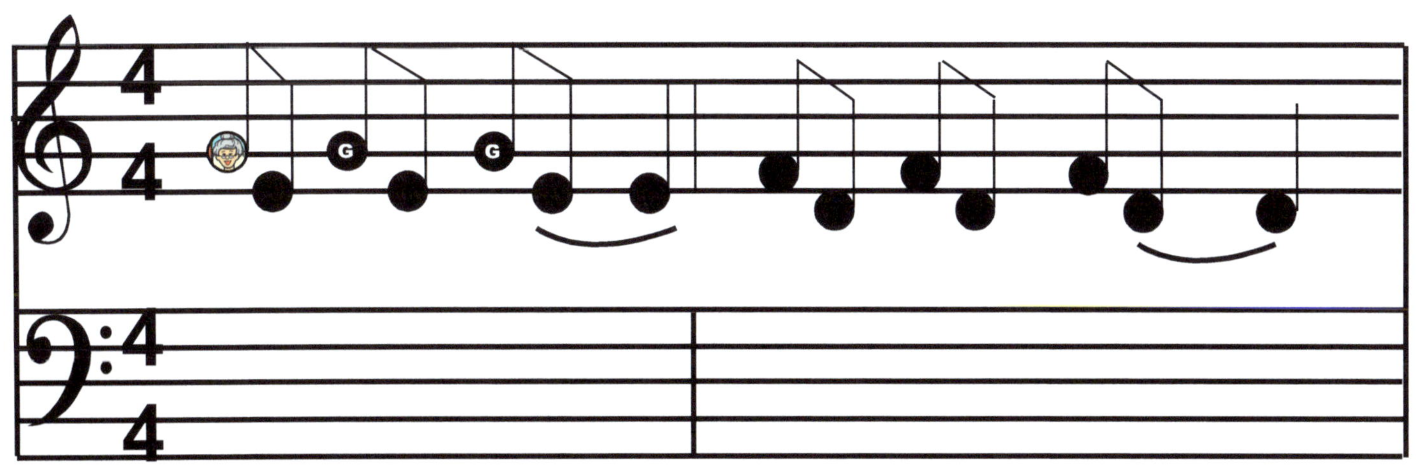

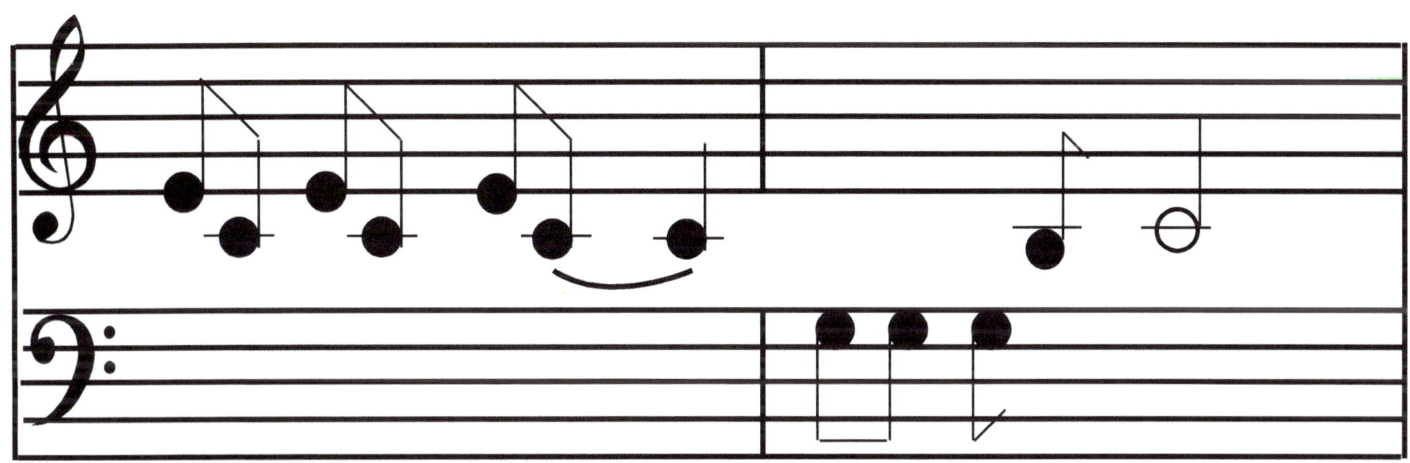

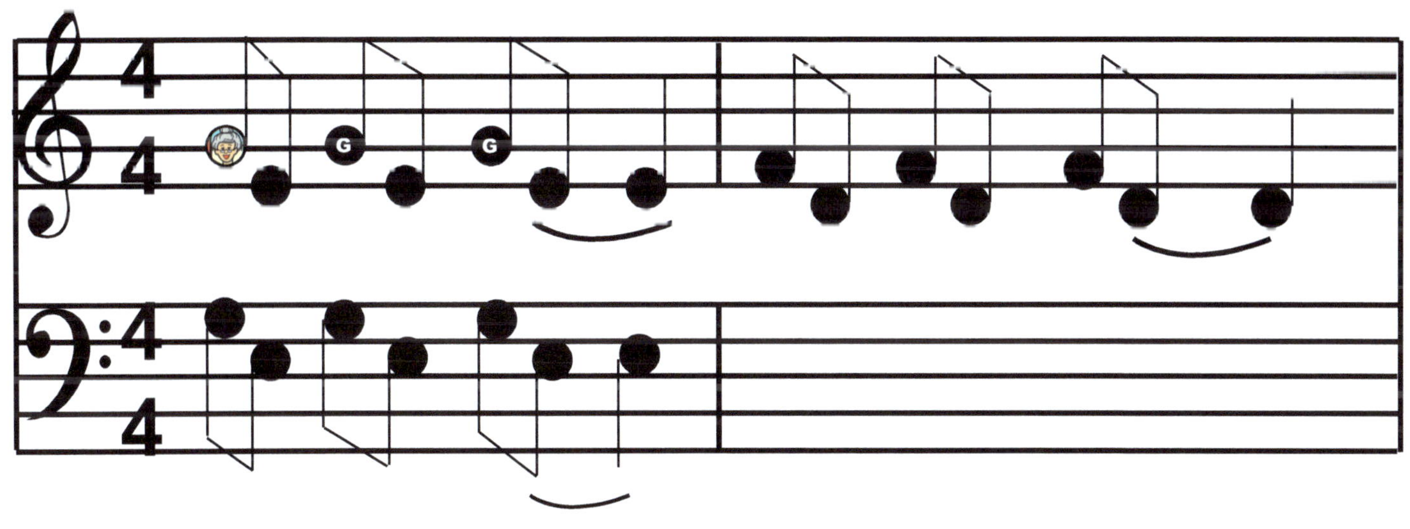

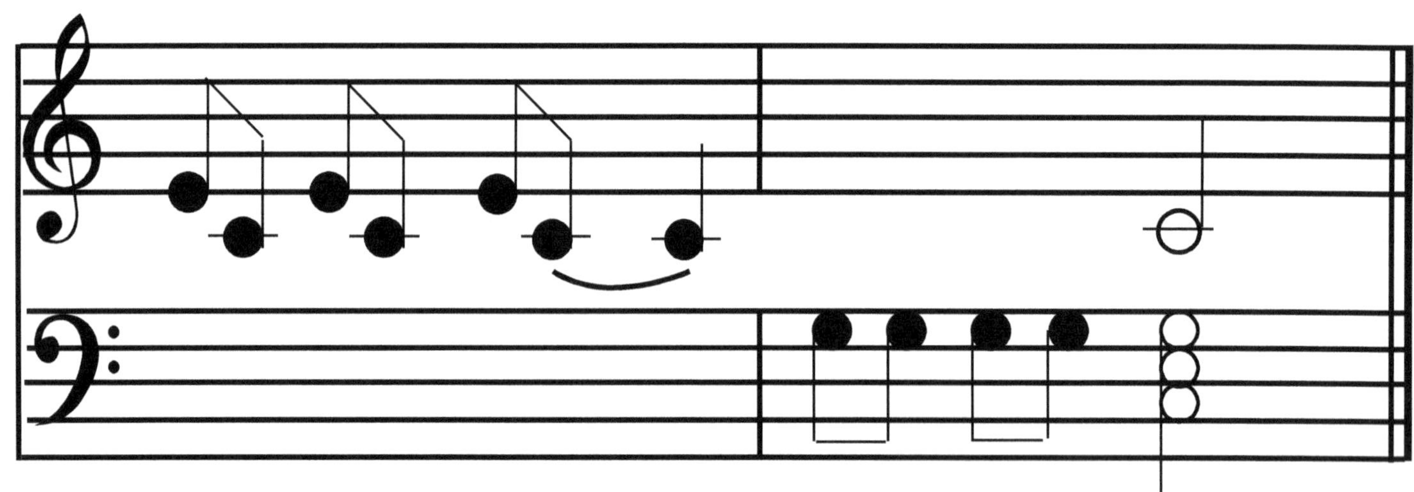

Dancing

E. Fredericks

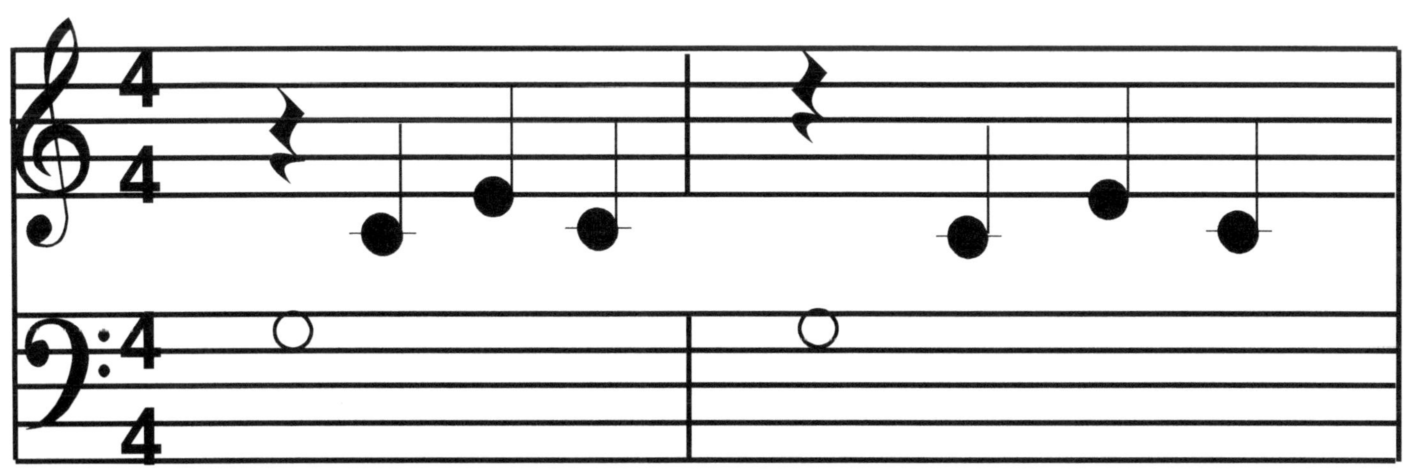

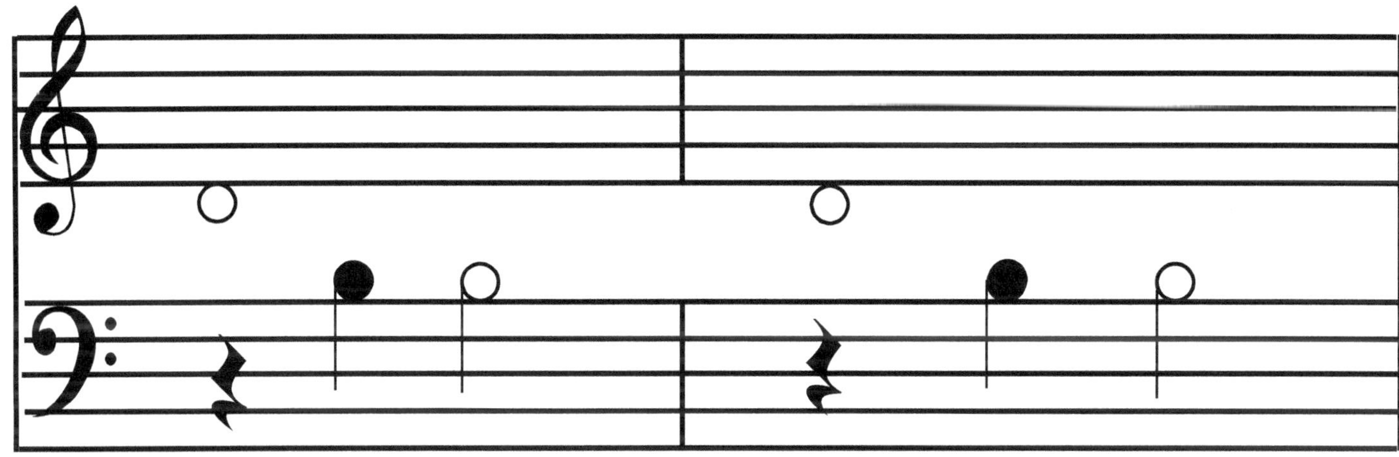

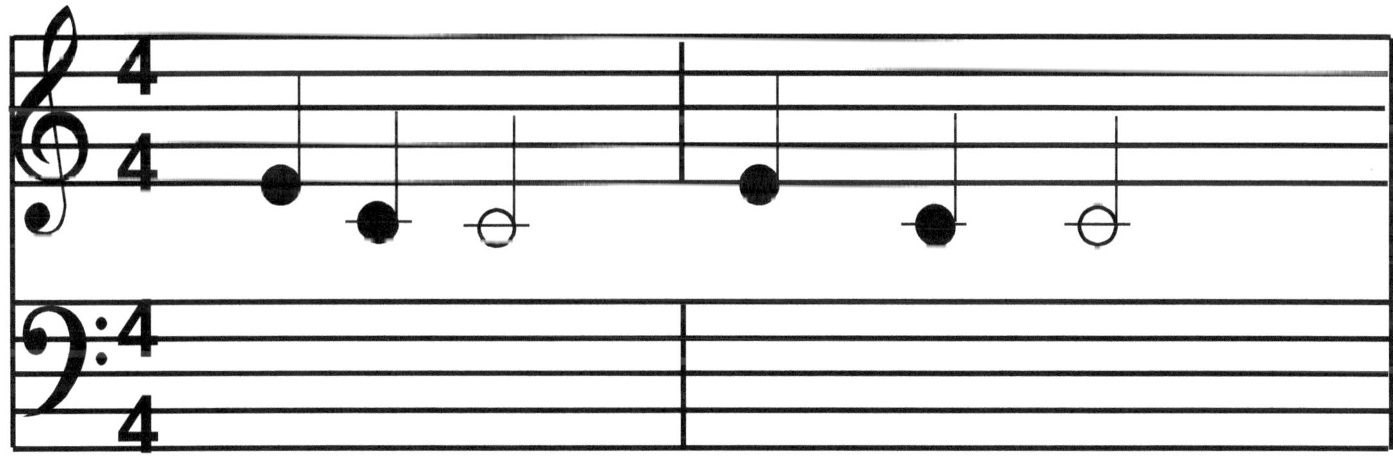

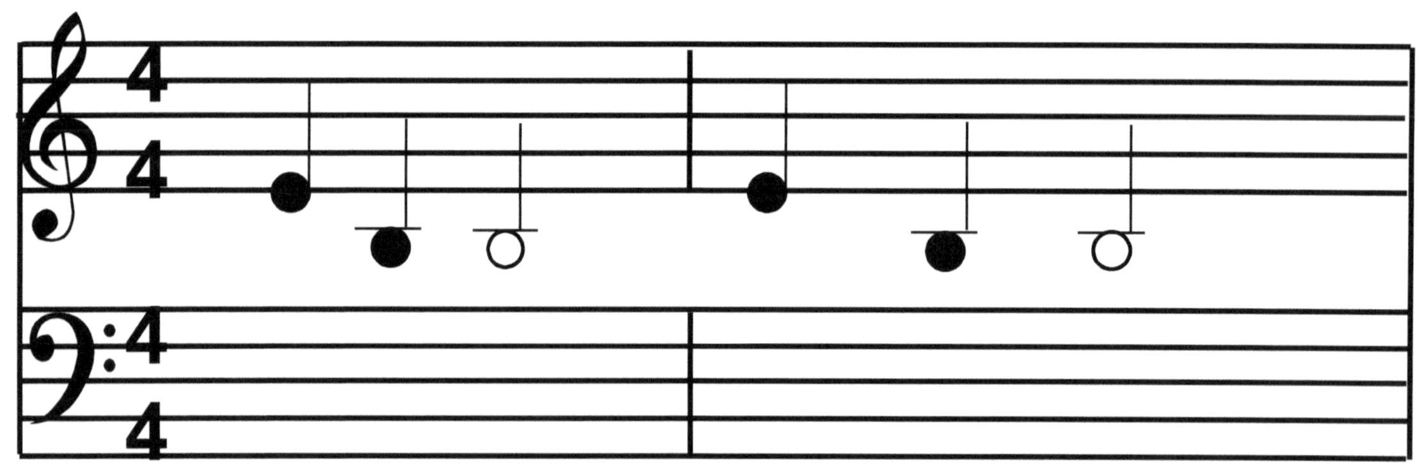

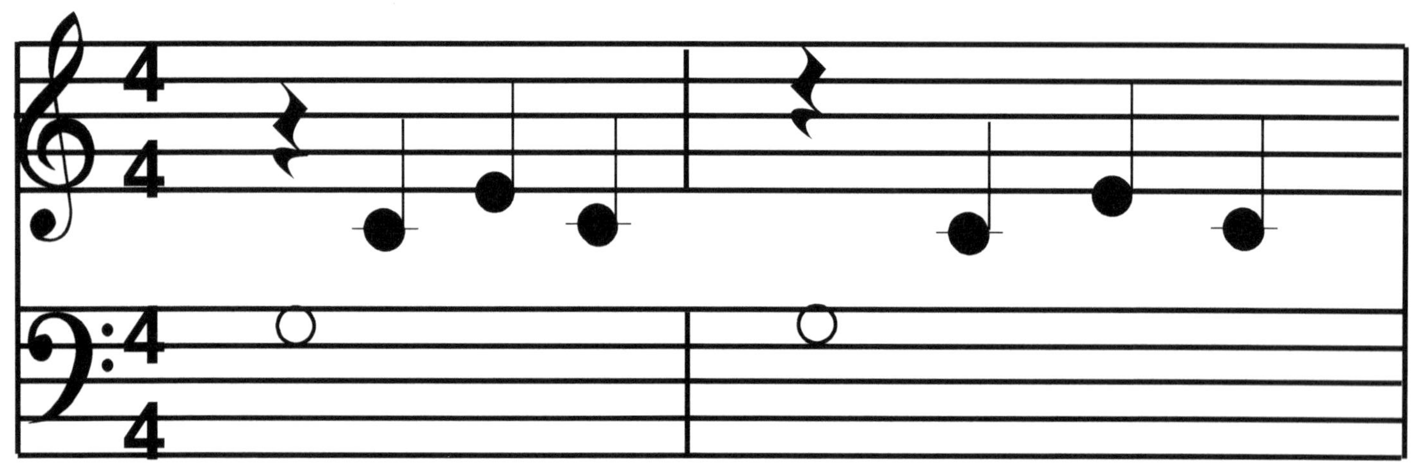

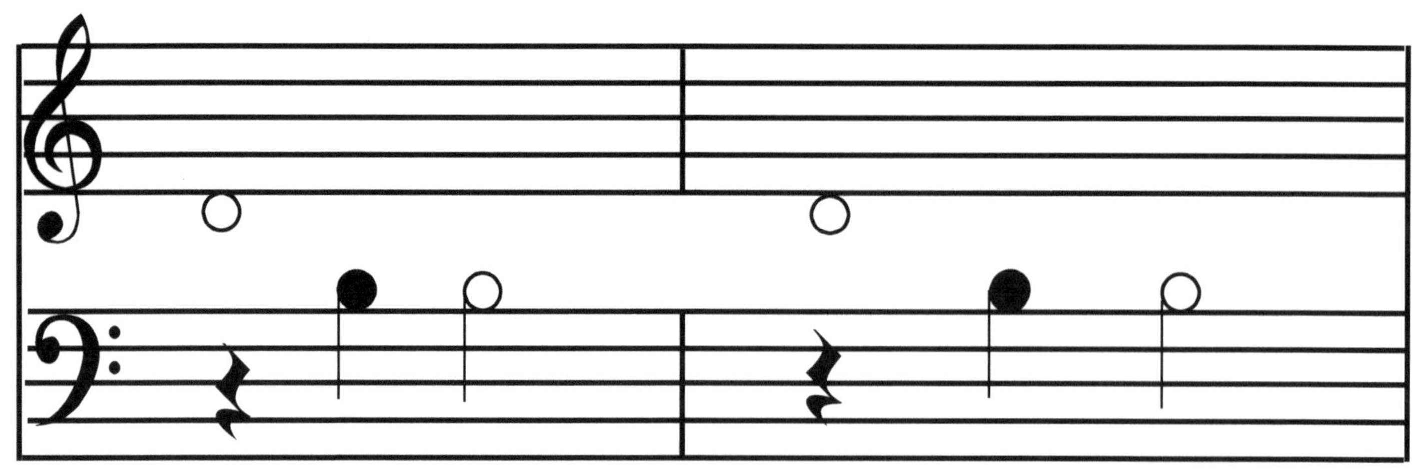

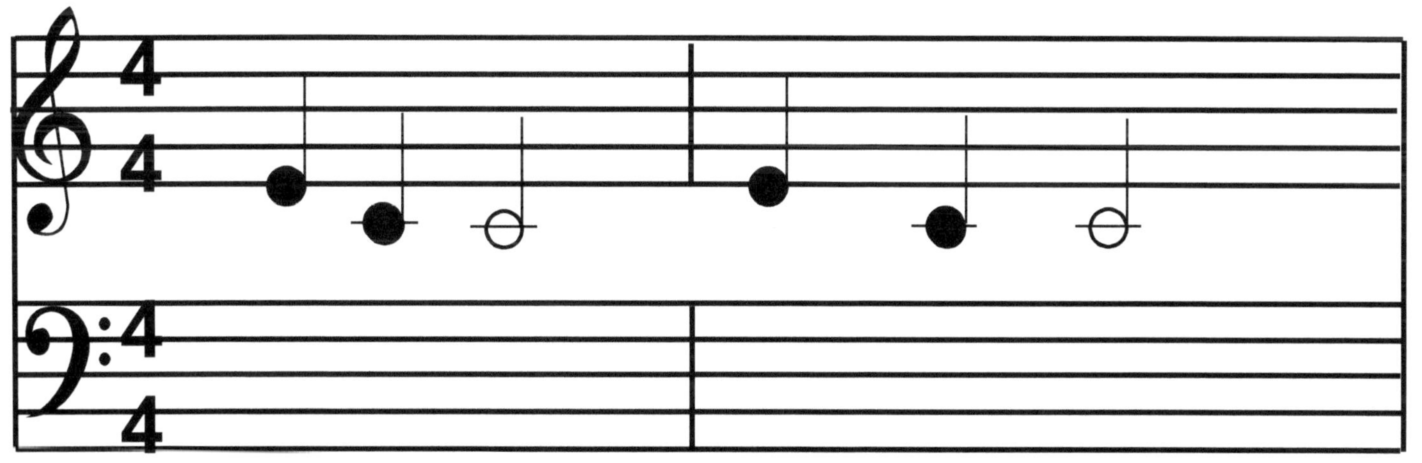

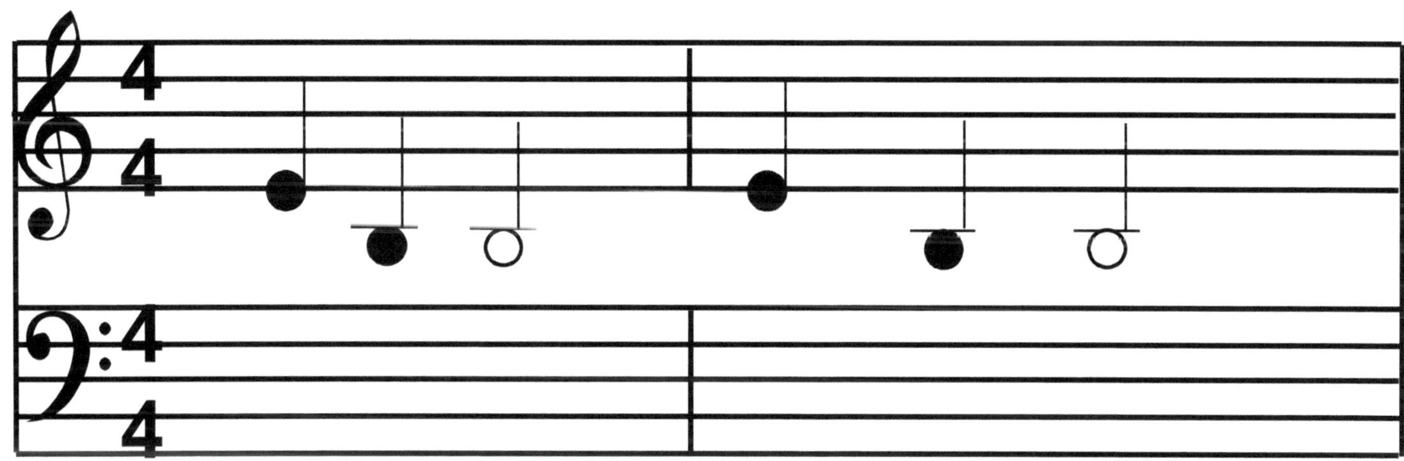

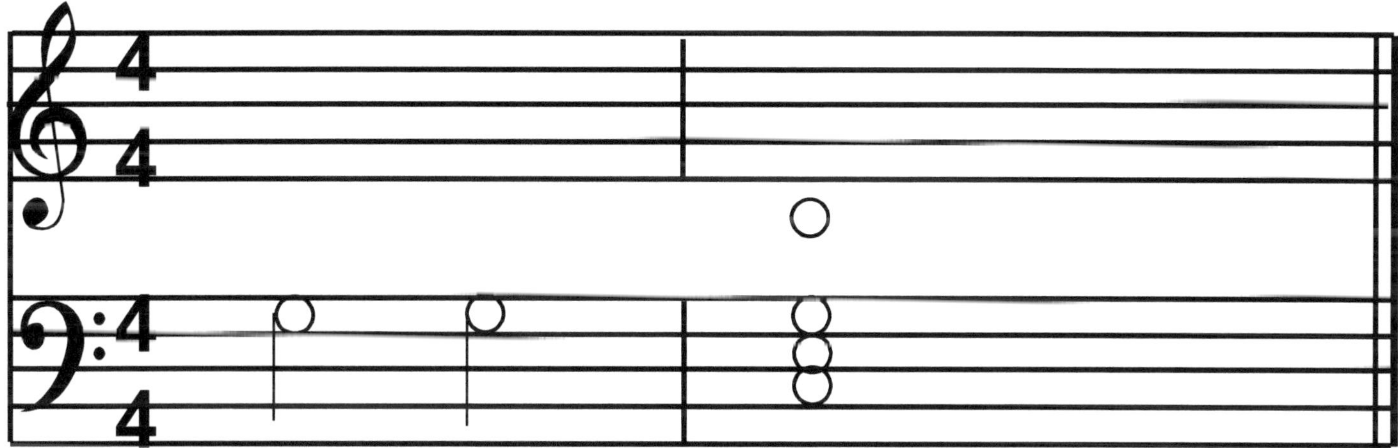

Raining

E. Fredericks

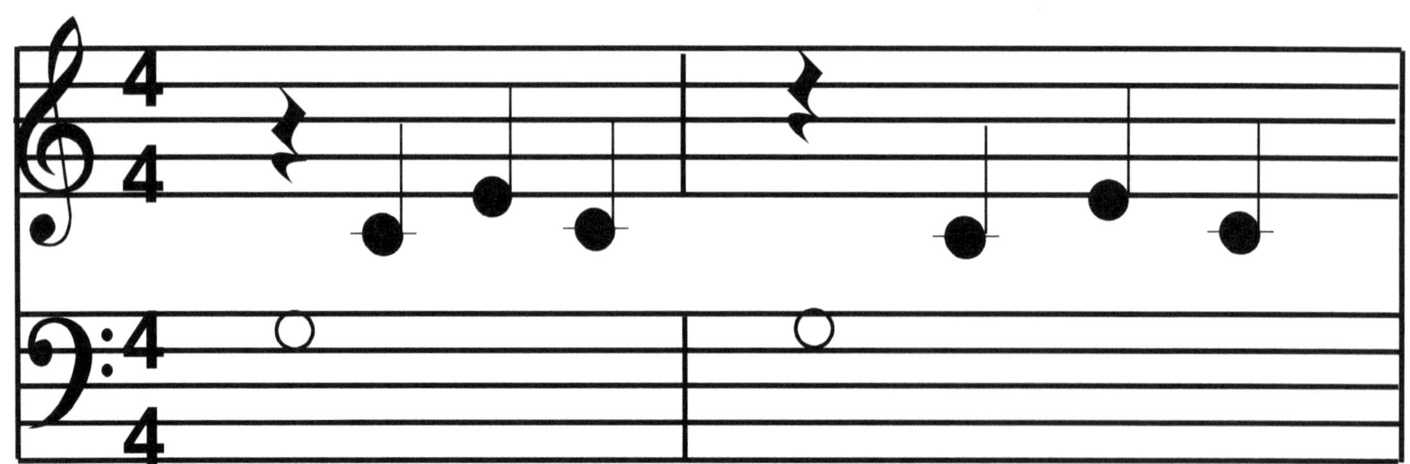

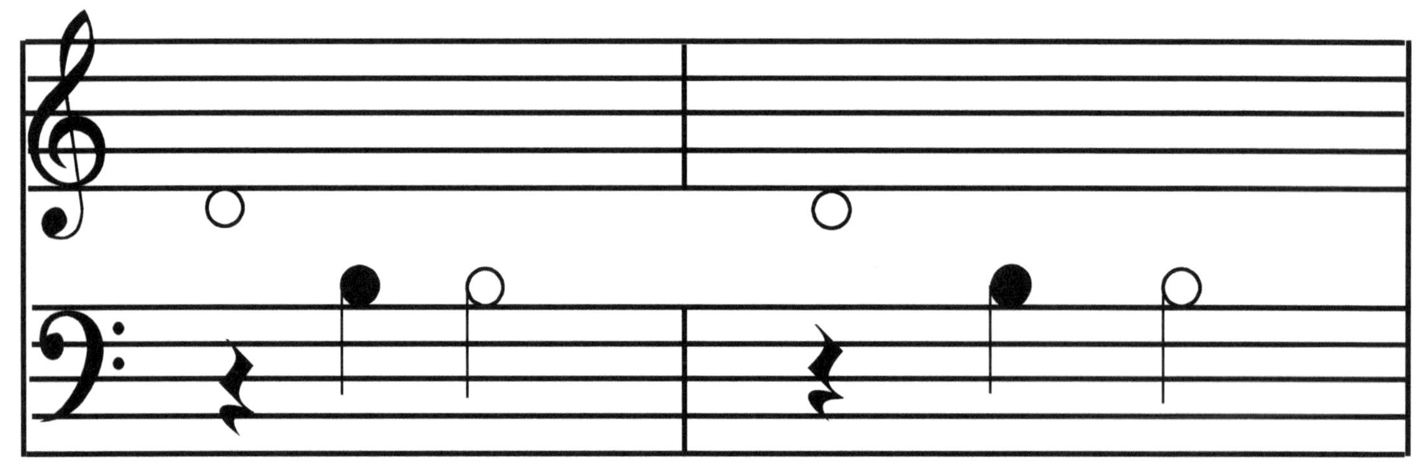

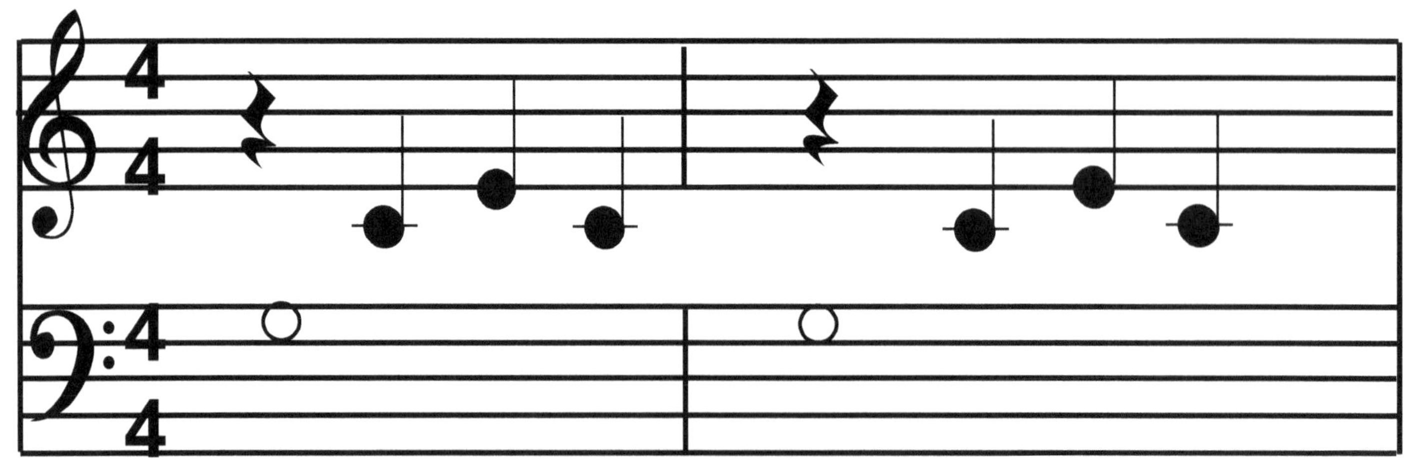

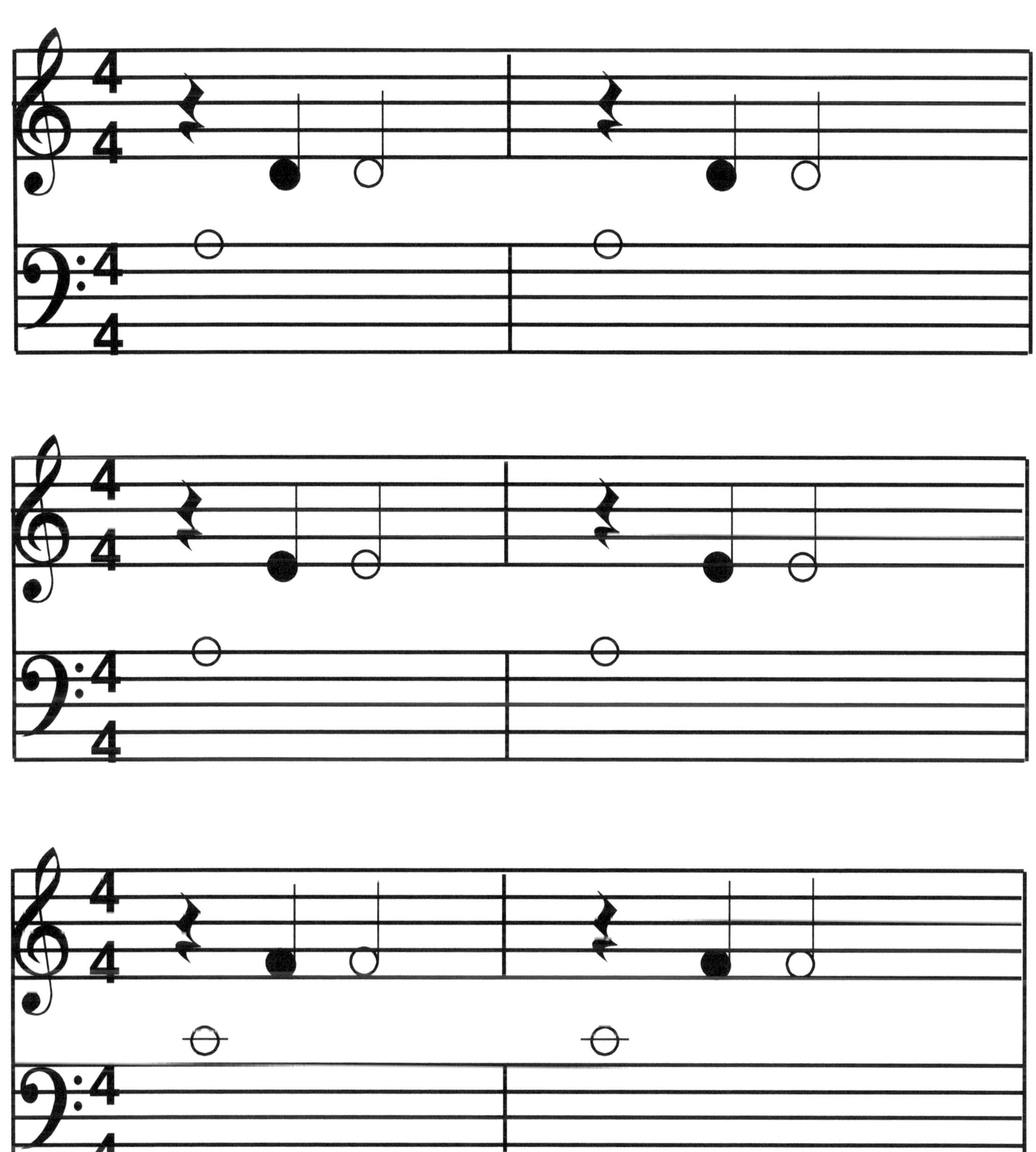

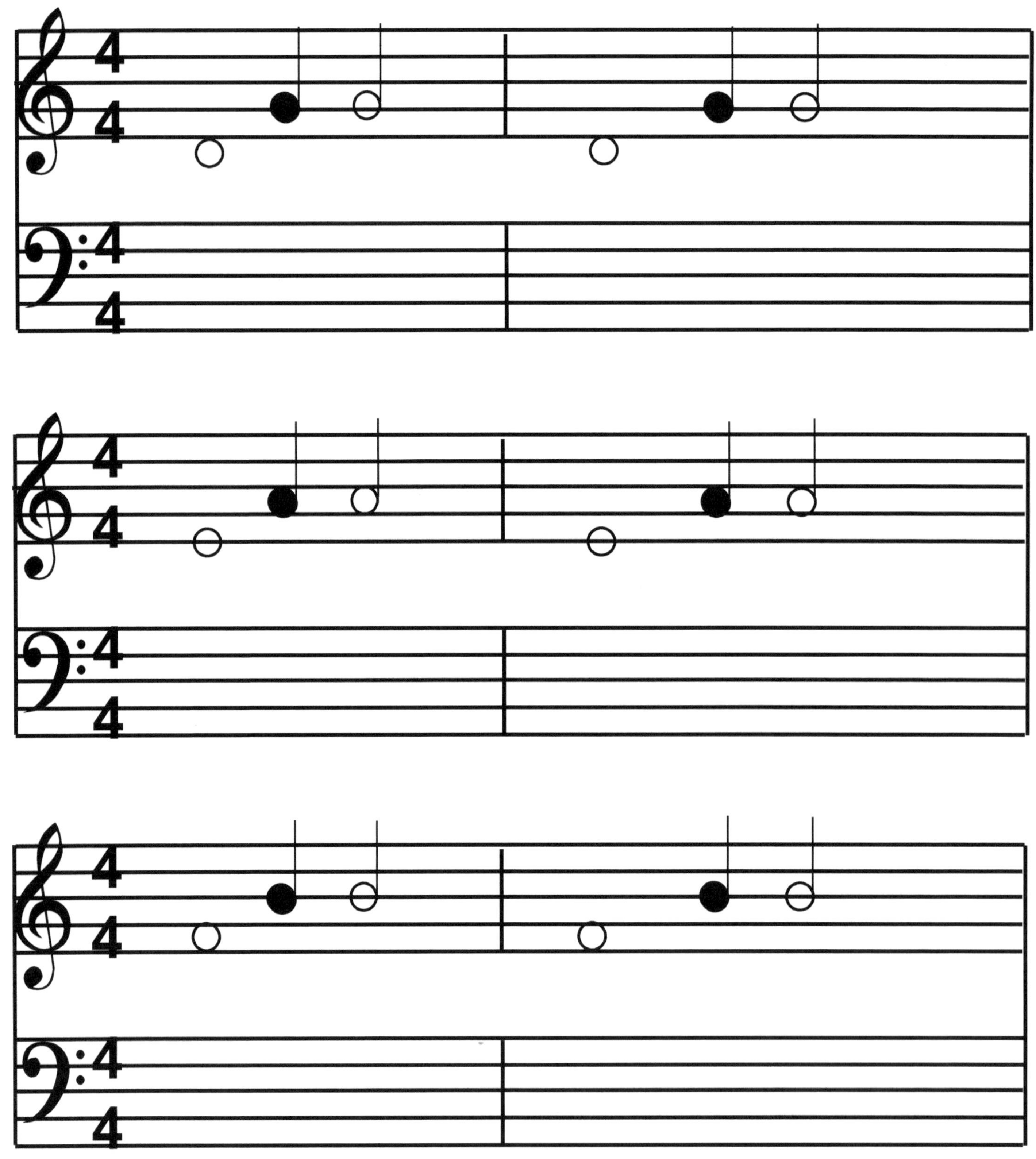

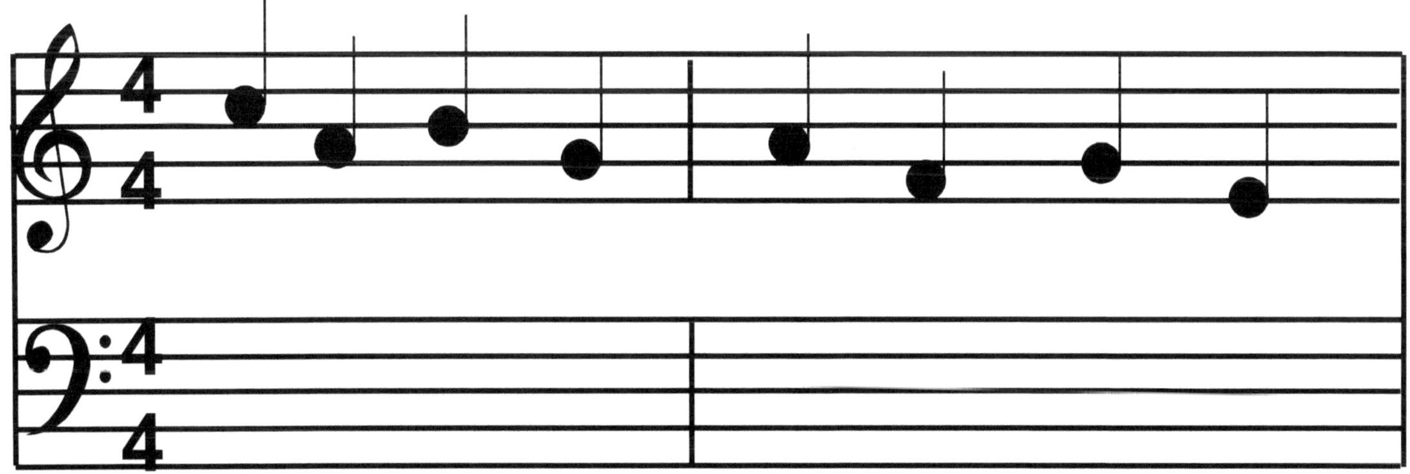

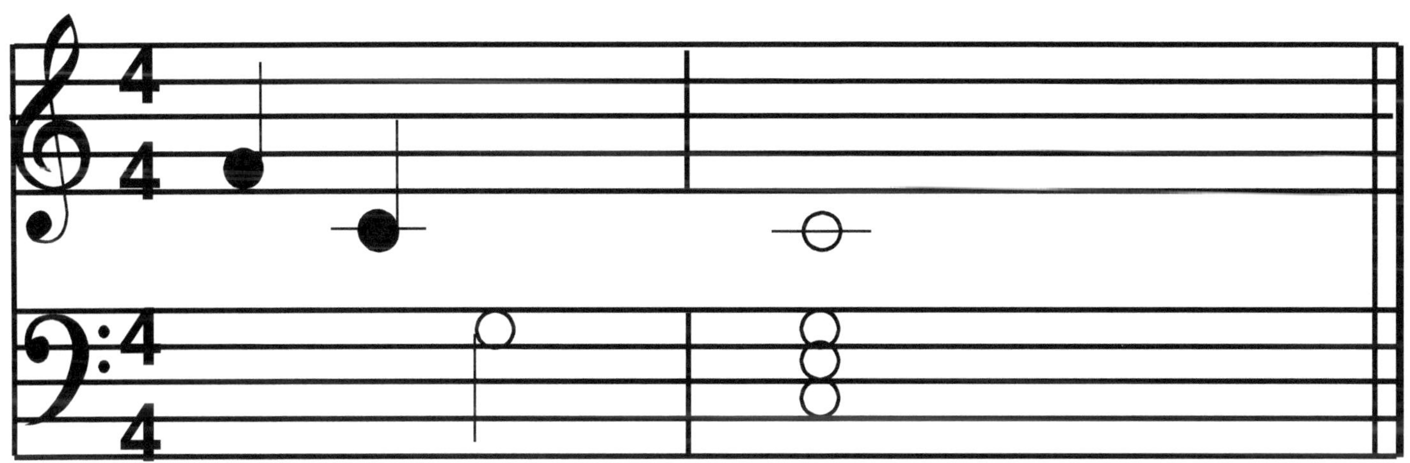

Amazing Grace

Evvie played this piece as a Father's Day gift for her dad on June 18, 2023.

Words by John Newton
Music by Carrell and Clayton

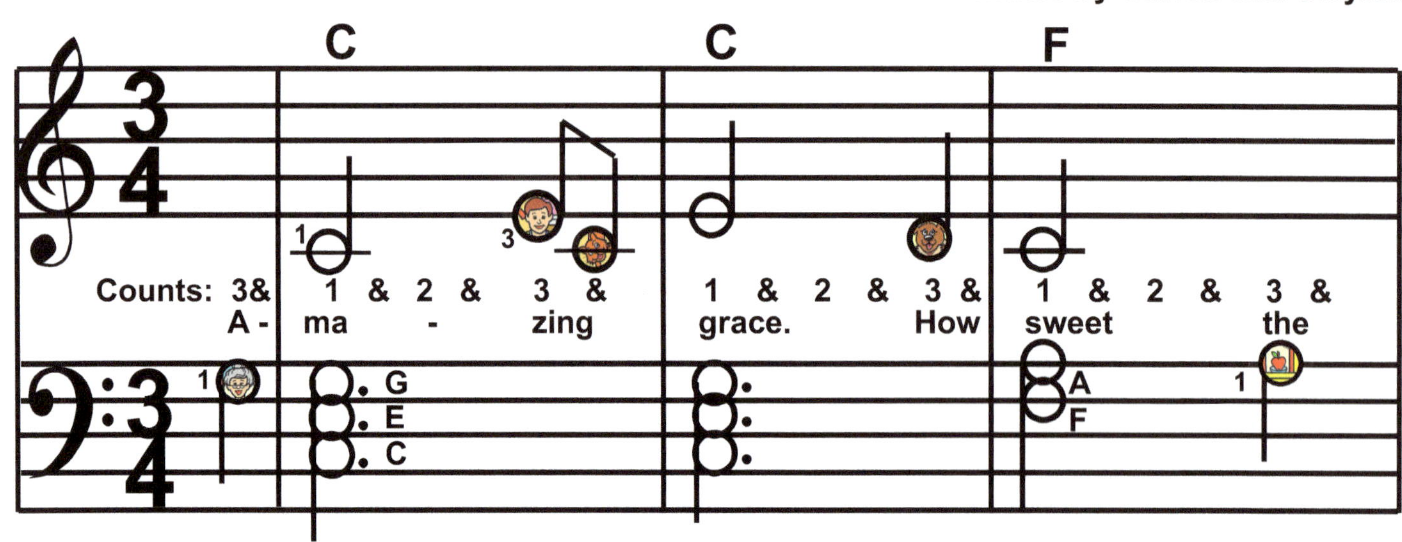

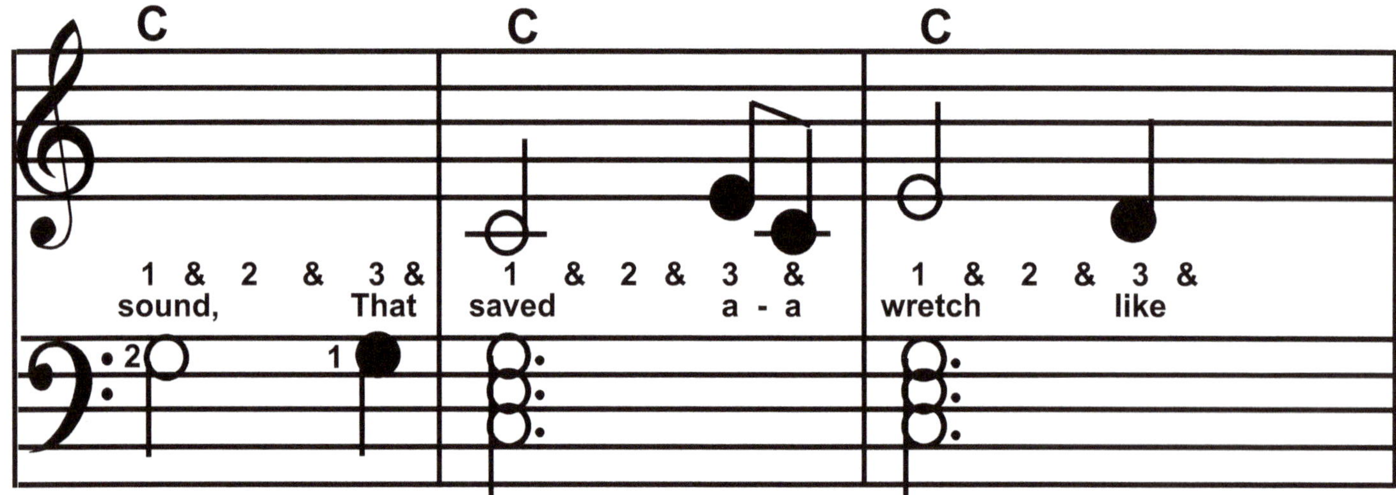

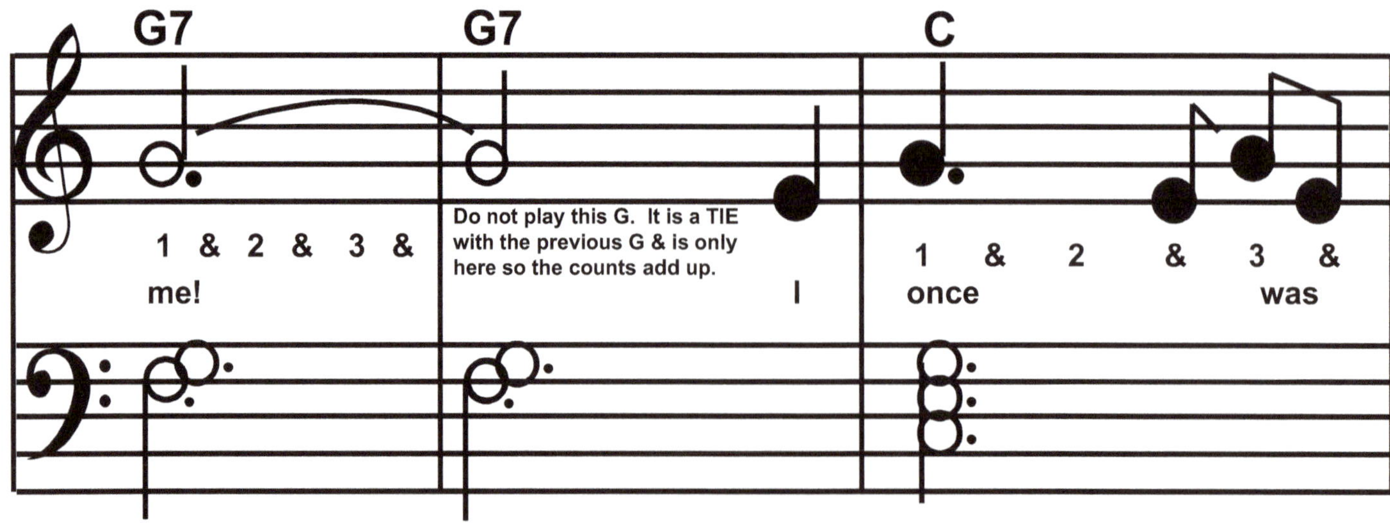

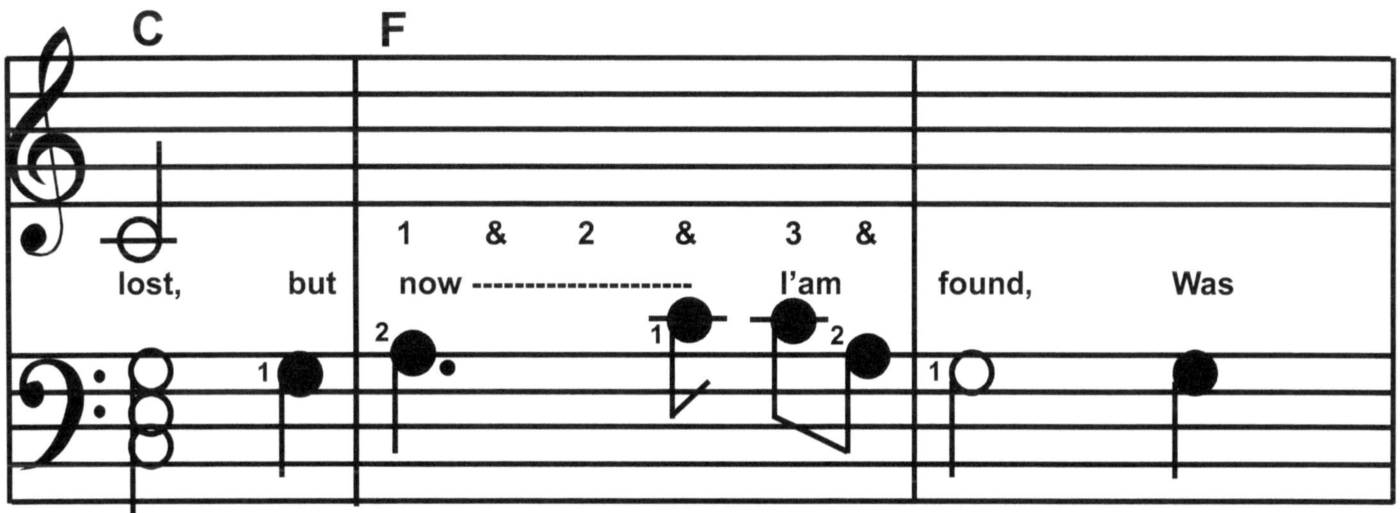

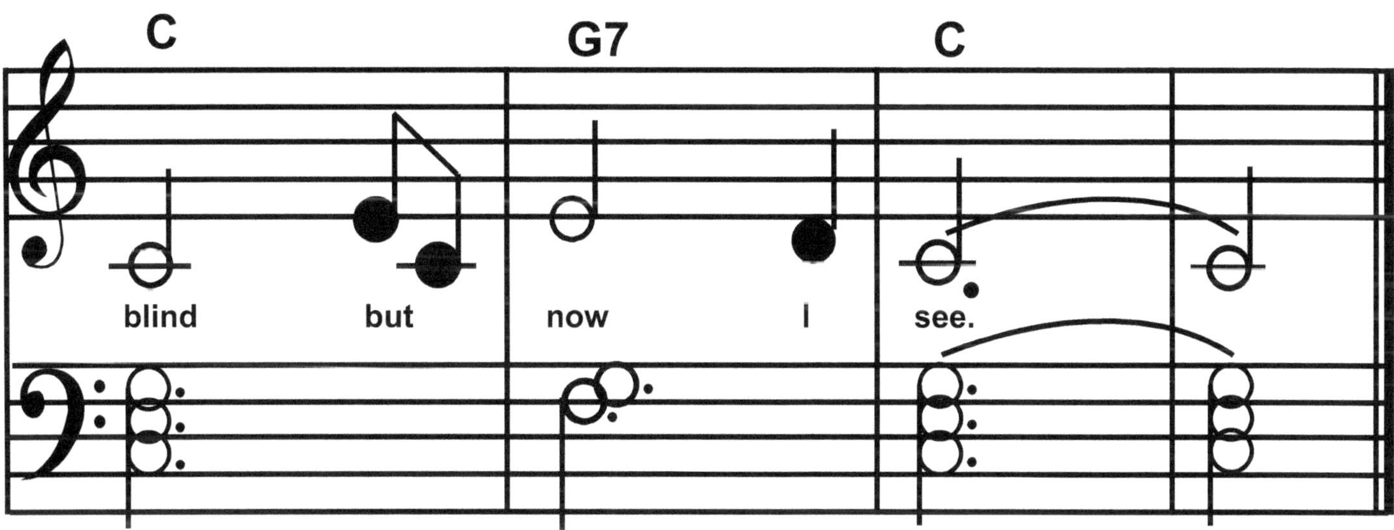

Verse 2 'Twas grace that taught my heart to fear
and grace my fears relieved;
How precious did that grace appear.
The hour I first believed.

Verse 3 Through many dangers, toils and snares
I have already come.
'Tis grace that brought me safe thus far,
And grace will lead me home.

Notice the new fingering in the left hand. This teaches you to cross your 2nd finger over the top of your first and back. The line between two notes which are the same note is called a tie. It tells you not to play the second note but to keep holding it until the next note is played. Watch your timing and counting.

Checklist for Composing

1.   Know where all the notes are on the musical staff.

2.   Decide how many counts you will place in each measure (or pizza box), and place the numbers on the musical staff after the clef signs. This is called the-time signature.

3.   Decide which scale you will use to write your song. If you are using a scale with sharps or flats, place these after the time signature. This is called the key signature.

4.   Think about the tune asking a question and then giving the answer. This is a common recipe for compositions.

5.   Decide if your piece will be loud, soft or a combination of these and put the symbols for these appropriately.

6.   Decide how you will include both hands in the piece and how you can in-clude chords. As you study chords in Picture Songs 2C, More Tricks, you will learn more about adding chords.

7.   End the song on the first note of the scale you have chosen so the song will sound finished to your ear.

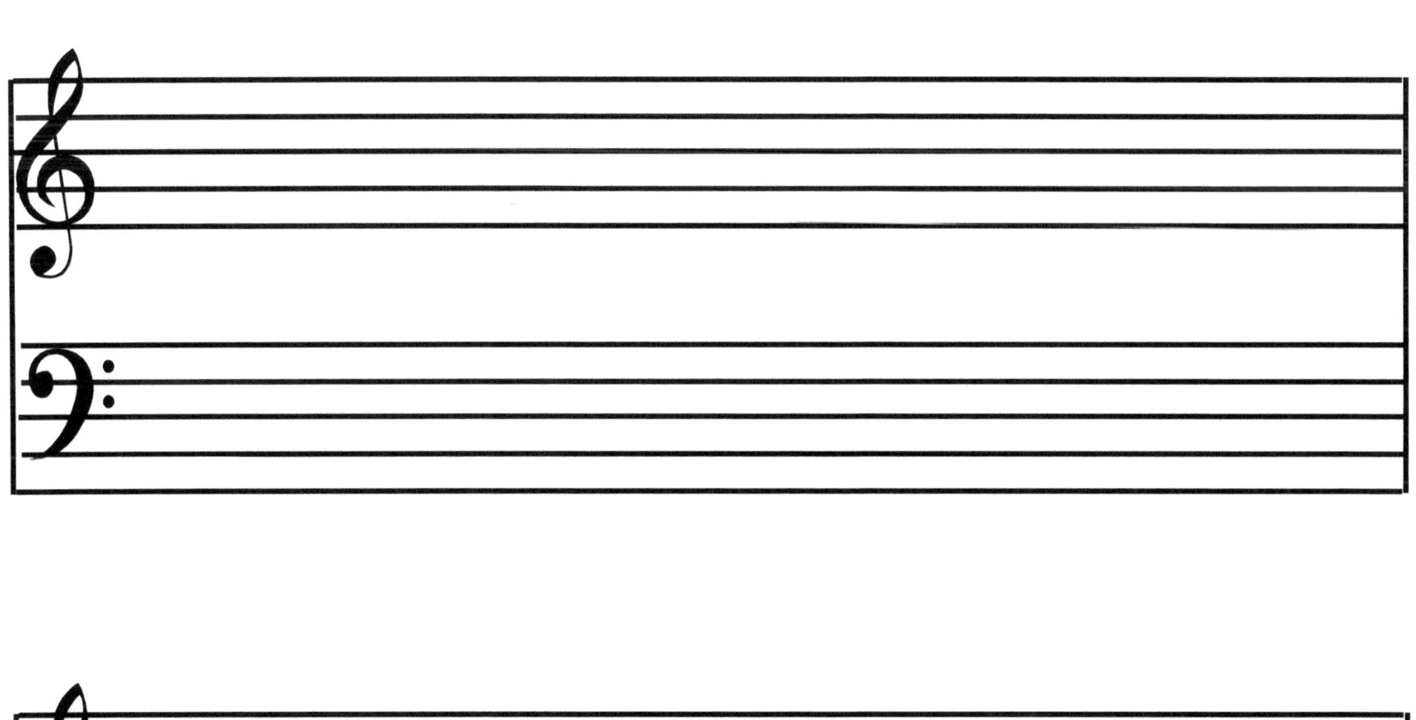
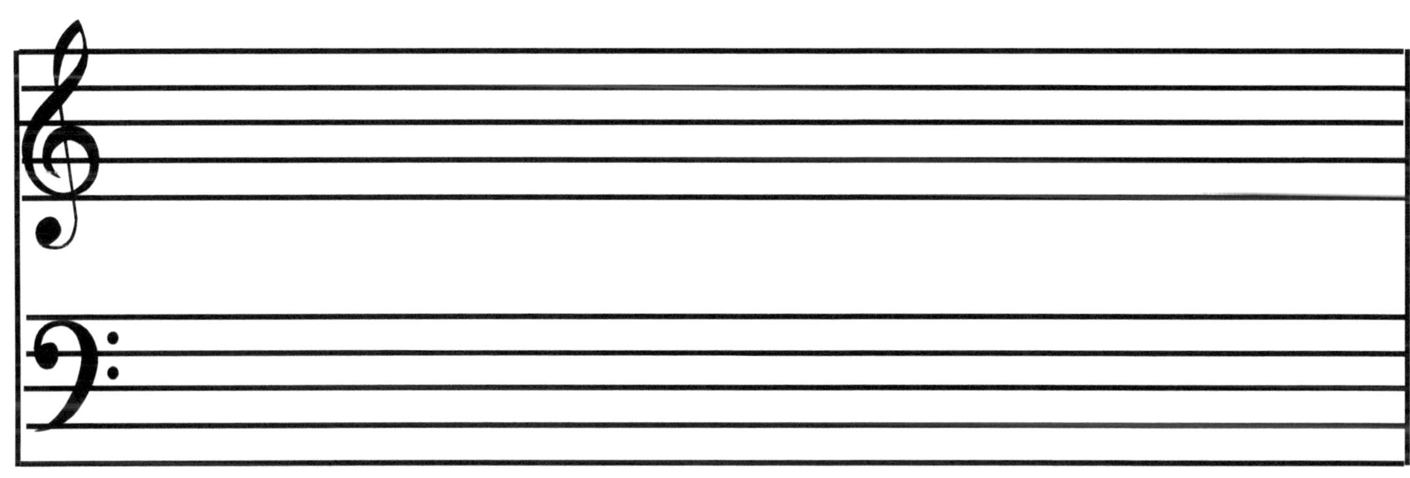
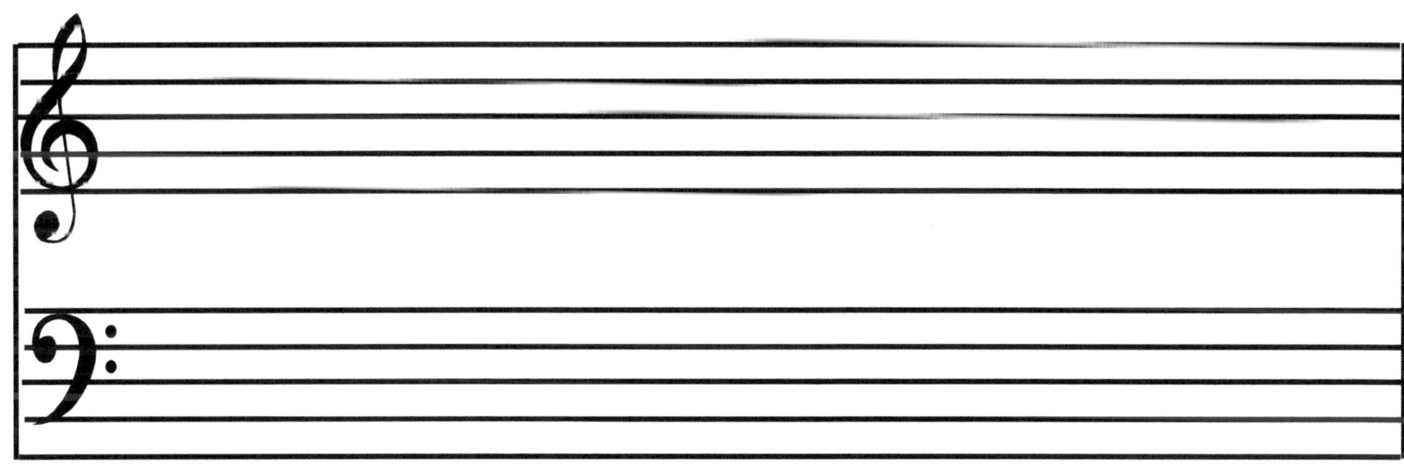

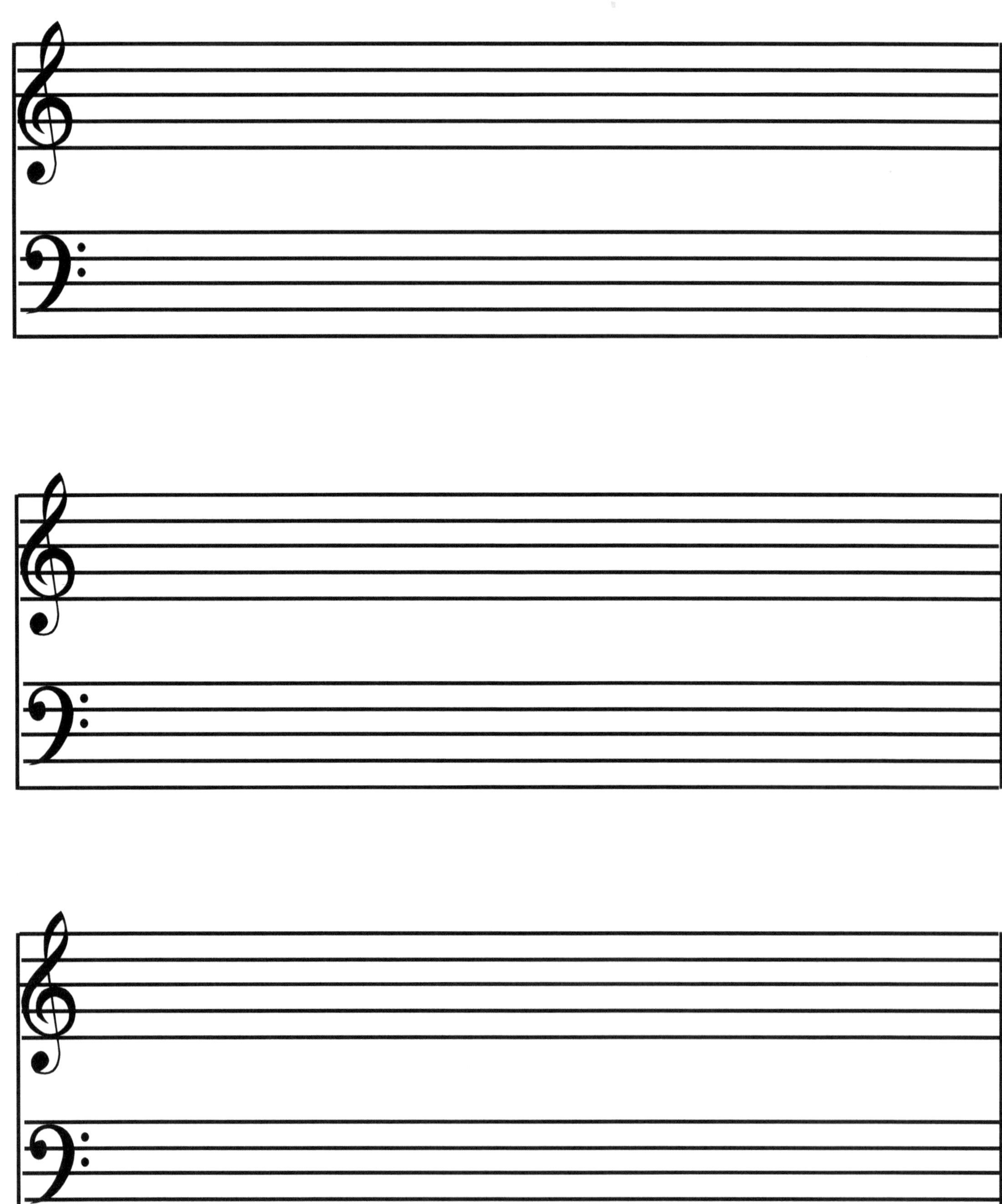

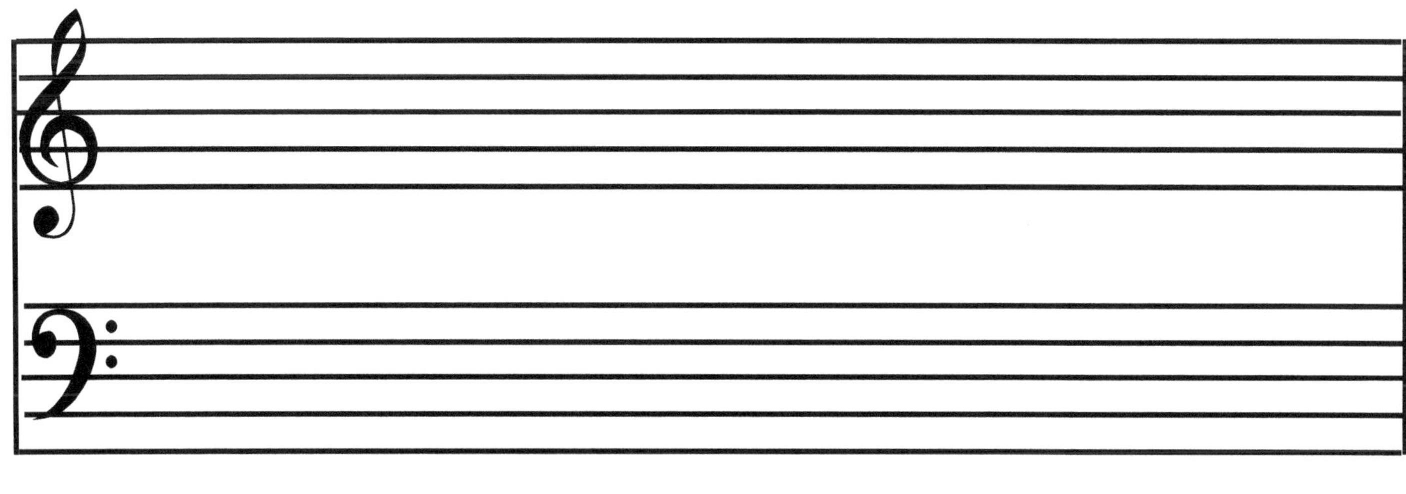

www.ingramcontent.com/pod-product-compliance
Lightning Source LLC
Chambersburg PA
CBHW040204240726
48664CB00002B/831